BURGUNDY

Compact Guide: Burgundy is the ideal quick-reference guide to this classic French destination. It tells you all you need to know about the region's attractions, from world-famous wines to medieval abbeys, high art to haute cuisine, and bustling markets to peaceful canal backwaters.

This is just one title in *Apa Publications'* new series of pocket-sized, easy-to-use guidebooks intended for the independent-minded traveller. *Compact Guides* pride themselves on being up-to-date and authoritative. They are in essence mini travel encyclopedias, designed to be comprehensive yet portable, as well as readable and reliable.

Star Attractions

An instant reference to some of Burgundy's most popular tourist attractions to help you on your way.

Dijon p16

Vercingetorix p47

Beaune p30

Wine cellars p33

Clos de Vougeot p38

Semur-en-Auxois p48

Fontenay Abbey p49

Auxerre p53

Cluny p64

Joigny market p56

Tournus p62

BURGUNDY

Introduction

Places

Culture

Leisure

Practical Information

Burgundy – Sunshine Trapped in a Bottle

Opposite: quality control

The musicians parade proudly, their caps, baggy red trousers, jackets and loose sleeves all brightly edged with green and yellow braid. Leading off with drums beating and trumpets, the spruced-up police band is followed by the town council, judges and other dignitaries, dressed in blue velvet and black hats with fluttering peacock feathers, by veiled noblewomen in swishing skirts and embroidered scarves, by fifers and drummers with gleaming coats-of-arms on their instruments, by blond-haired page boys in high-heeled shoes and by escorts on prancing horses. And the people stand and stare as the procession in all its splendour progresses down the street to receive the Duke of Burgundy and his retinue on the edge of town. A Duke of Burgundy? But surely centuries have passed since they were the rulers in these parts? Perhaps this is part of *Les Trois Glorieuses*, one of the Three Glorious Days that marks the end of the Côte d'Or grape harvest. The trouble is that in Burgundy it can sometimes be hard to distinguish the past and the present.

For over a century Burgundy was ruled by four dukes. At that time it was a flourishing and expanding empire with grand ambitions, a courtly society residing in Dijon, with Flemish artists and influential abbeys, a citadel of spirituality and art.

White Charolais beef herds graze the peaceful pastures, wrinkled vine-growers tend their grapes under the baking sun and mobile butchers keep the villages supplied with provisions. But the signs of a glorious past are visible everywhere in the green and hilly countryside: on the slopes of Mont Auxois where Caesar's troops defeated the Gallic chieftain Vercingetorix and opened a new chapter in European history, against the backdrop of medieval chivalry in Semur-en-Auxois, in the captivating monuments of the Romanesque period, in Dijon's aristocratic old town, on the tranquil canals between the Loire and the Saône or in the untidy workshop of a clog factory in the mountainous Morvan.

Even during a four-course evening meal in the heart of medieval Beaune, within sight of the Ducal Palace in Dijon or by the banks of the Yonne in Auxerre, history is never far away. A glass of deep red burgundy may well accompany the *boeuf bourguignon* – the same wine that was served at the court of the French kings in Versailles.

Situation and landscape

Unlike many other parts of France, this region, situated at the very heart of the country, is not a clearly defined entity; it is, in fact, a tapestry of many varied landscapes: valleys, plains, uplands and mountains. With an area of

Aristocratic Dijon

A tempting tipple

5

Rural idyll

Harvest time approaches
The mythical Morvan

32,000sq km (12,350sq miles), Burgundy covers some 6 percent of France and is roughly the same size as Belgium or South Carolina. The Champagne region lies to the north, the Jura and Franche-Comté to the east, Beaujolais and the Lyonnais in the south and the Loire Valley in the west. Dissected by a series of deep valleys, the Morvan hills dominate the centre of the region like a natural fortress. This outcrop of crystalline rocks including granite, porphyry and gneiss forms the eastern edge of the Massif Central and has only limited value as farmland. Haut-Folin (901m/ 2,995ft), Mont Préneley (855m/2,804ft) and Mont Beuvray (821m/2,692ft) are the highest peaks in Burgundy. Two lower ranges run in a north-south direction parallel to the Saône Valley: the famous wine-producing Côte d'Or and the Mâconnais, which links up with the Beaujolais area further south.

Although it lies in the east of the region, the Saône Valley, together with the limestone Côte d'Or uplands between the region's capital of Dijon and the smaller rural town of Autun, forms the historic heart of Burgundy. In the Dijonnais, as it is called, every type of landscape is represented, so this corner of Burgundy serves as a good starting point.

Although much is heavily cultivated, other parts of Burgundy are densely wooded. The Morvan hills, in particular, have yielded many myths and legends. The word *morvan* derives from the Celtic and means 'black mountain'. A number of rivers such as the Yonne, Cure, Cousin and Serein rise in the Morvan range and flow northwards, while the Arroux, Bourbince and Arronce flow into the Loire and the Ouche, Dheune and Grosne into the Saône, the Rhône's main tributary. In the north of the region on the Langres plateau lies the source of the Seine which flows northwards through Paris and into the Atlantic, but the Armançon and Ozerain also eventually reach the Atlantic, beginning their path northwards on the chalky but deeply furrowed Auxois plain.

The canals of Burgundy

As well as the scores of natural watercourses, the region also boasts many pretty canals. They were dug in the 18th century when France was developing as an industrial power, but are now of little commercial value. The Canal du Centre is the only one which still has any significant amount of business traffic, but not enough to disturb its tranquil scenery. These often shaded waterways have, in recent years, become very popular with tourists who enjoy taking to the water. Gently chugging through the Burgundy countryside on a canal must rank as one of the most relaxing ways to take a holiday. With a maximum permitted speed of 8kmph (5mph), even cyclists on the towpath will overtake the canal boats and as the waterways in Burgundy are blocked by no fewer than 558 locks, progress is, by necessity, slow. The faint-hearted may well be deterred by such a number, if not by the detailed instructions provided by the boat-hire company, but after a dozen or so attempts, negotiating lock gates usually becomes a simple task. Nothing moves in or out of the locks after 7.30pm anyway.

The Rhine-Rhône Canal connects Dijon with the Rhine and the opening of the Canal de la Marne à la Saône linked the region with Paris. The Canal de Bourgogne, built between 1775 and 1834, winds its way through Burgundy for 242km (150 miles) and the Canal du Nivernais, which was completed in 1842, meanders from the Yonne to the Loire. The main commercial role for these waterways was in the transportation of timber and wine.

Burgundy's canal and river network exceeds 2,000km (1,250 miles) in length and it provides a splendid opportunity to enjoy both the pleasures of rural France and the cultural richness of Burgundy's urban centres (contact the French tourist board for further information, *see page 86*).

Climate and when to go

Given its central location, the region naturally enjoys a continental climate with clear seasonal differences. In high summer, it can be so hot that the only way to keep cool is to take a dip in one of the many lakes or head up into the Morvan hills. In winter, though, it can be bitterly cold and a glass or two of something warming is sometimes required. The weather fronts usually approach from the west, and if the moisture-laden clouds on their way from the Atlantic are slow-moving, then that invariably means a steady downpour in the geographical heart of the region.

In the southern *département* of Saône-et-Loire, however, spring often arrives at the end of February with blossoming vegetation and warm temperatures. The warmer temperatures spread northwards up the broad Rhône Valley from the Mediterranean coast via Lyon and, by March, café proprietors in Mâcon will be starting to arrange their tables and chairs outside in the sunshine. But take care in the hilly upland regions in central Burgundy. Even in March the meadows here will be covered with frost first thing in the morning.

Burgundy makes an ideal year-round destination. In the depths of winter, many hardy souls enjoy tours around the churches, monasteries, fortresses and *châteaux*, although admittedly it is more fun in the warmer months. Autumn is a very popular time of year, as conditions are bright and sunny, but not too hot for touring. However, early

Taking to the water

7

Windsurfing on Lac des Settons

morning mists may put a damper on some sightseeing. Rainfall levels are highest in October (and also May and June) but the changing leaf colour on the vines and trees creates a beautiful spectacle. At this time of year, the farmers are busy in their vineyards harvesting their precious crop and on the Côte d'Or, in the Chalonnais, the Mâconnais and Chablis, there is much to be done.

Nature and environment

Anyone starting a tour of Burgundy in Dijon and then heading south could be forgiven for thinking that every square yard of soil is given over to wine production. It is true that most of the land is cultivated, but grapes are not the only crop. The four Burgundian administrative units still have large expanses of natural terrain, with most of it found in the Morvan hills where the four *départements* meet. In addition, over 1,000 springs flow from the hillsides. Some feed the larger rivers and lakes, while others are dammed to create reservoirs such as Lac des Settons. This has not only developed into a popular recreational area but also guarantees good supplies of drinking water and maintains, along with other reservoirs, the levels of nearby rivers during dry periods. Most of these lakes are situated in the Parc Naturel Régional de Morvan. It was established in 1970 and covers an area of 1,700sq km (656sq miles). When it was opened, nature conservation was not a major consideration. More important from the 35,000 inhabitants' point of view was the need to stimulate tourism and to encourage agricultural development and forestry.

Large parts of the park are covered with meadows and pastures, bordered by both broadleaf and pine woodland. Ivy often clings to the tree trunks and, in the more open spaces, celandine and white and blue dog violets thrive.

At higher altitudes the slopes are adorned with lilac-coloured pasque flowers. The region is also rich in wildlife. Deer, badgers, foxes, hares, rabbits and rodents frequently cross the footpaths while, in the lakes and rivers, trout, carp, pike and zander are plentiful. Above the tree-tops hover hawks, buzzards, peregrine falcons and other birds of prey. The Morvan hills are also a rich source of mushrooms, many of which find their way on to the plates of diners in Burgundian restaurants. Gourmets should look for ceps, chanterelles and morels.

The numerous cave systems are among Burgundy's natural wonders. The best-known complex is the 6-km (4-mile) long Grottes d'Arcy near Vézelay where for millions of years the River Cure has been eroding the limestone strata. The Grande Grotte, with its bizarre stalactites and stalagmites and an underground lake, is the highlight of this system. Like the Grottes d'Arcy, the impressive Grottes de Blanot, to the northeast of Cluny, were inhabited by early man.

For those who prefer the open air, the Rochers du Saussois are worth a visit. Separated from the Canal du Nivernais by the motorway and a row of houses, these grey-white chalk rocks present a challenge to rock-climbers at all times of the year.

Population and religion

Of all the French regions, only Corsica and the Limousin have a lower population density. While the average density for the whole of France is 104 people per square kilometre, in Burgundy there are on average only 51 in the same area. While 26 percent of the French population as a whole live off the land, almost half of all Burgundians depend on the soil. But it is not fair to regard Burgundy as a backward provincial region. Admittedly, the most thinly-populated Nièvre *département* has suffered badly in the past few decades with many young people leaving for the towns. This eastern part of the region on the edge of the Morvan hills can offer only poor employment prospects. Only Nevers can boast any industry and the average age of Nièvre's inhabitants is much higher than elsewhere – some 28 percent are over the age of 60.

The Côte d'Or, on the other hand, is not just a wealthy *département* but, with the city of Dijon at its heart, relatively densely populated. In no way is this conurbation a monster smothered by exhaust emissions and tarnished by industrial complexes; instead, it has the air of a rather well-heeled, sophisticated aristocrat, who enjoys worldly pleasures as much as the fine arts. This major city blends easily with an agricultural region steeped in tradition.

There is an uneven distribution of industry in Burgundy, reflecting the differing population densities of the four *dé-*

At the market in Mâcon
Growing up in Chalon

Devotions at Paray-le-Monial

partements. When the industrialisation process started in the 19th century, many of the new workers came from outside Burgundy and, by 1881, the population had risen to 1.76 million, 150,000 more than today. In the first half of the 20th century, however, the numbers fell, reaching their lowest level between 1945 and 1950. Since then, the population has risen slightly, levelling out at today's 1.6 million. As a result of its unfavourable economic circumstances and casualties during both world wars, the Nièvre *département* lost just under 26 percent of its population, whereas in Saône-et-Loire the decline was 18 percent and in Yonne 17 percent.

Visitors to Burgundy's important monastery sites such as Cluny and Paray-le-Monial may well gain the impression that the people of Burgundy are all devout Catholics, but on closer examination that turns out to be not quite the case. In the Charolais to the south, the people have always been loyal followers of the Church of Rome, but in the Yonne *département* a strong anticlerical feeling exists.

Tradition and customs

As in the rest of France, time has not stood still during the past 200 years. The tractor is now firmly established as a vital tool in the modern vineyard and it is rare to see a cigarette-puffing, beret-wearing peasant farmer tending his vines with a hoe these days.

Nevertheless, traditions and customs are still firmly embedded in the Burgundian way of life and some of these probably date from Celtic times. With the advent of Christianity in the 4th century, these were incorporated into the religious calendar. In some areas, bundles of brushwood are left leaning against doors in the spring to keep the ever-present evil spirits away. When moving, soup is sometimes sprinkled around the houses.

Les Trois Glorieuses (Three Glorious Days) is one of Burgundy's most famous annual events. This festival dates from 1830 when the people celebrated the July revolution, but over the years it has evolved into three separate wine festivals which take place after the grape harvest during the last weekend in November. At the Clos du Vougeot on the Saturday, the order of the Chevaliers du Tastevin hold an extravagant meeting known as a *chapitre*. This event is followed on the Sunday by an auction of the Hospices de Beaune wines. The finale, the La Paulée wine festival, takes place on the Monday in Meursault.

Economy

Although Burgundy is not a clearly defined geographical entity, in a commercial sense it is a homogeneous region. But it is this factor which, in the opinion of many economists, causes some of the problems for the region.

Knight of the Tastevin, Clos de Vougeot

Southern Burgundy, which includes Mâcon, looks further south towards the Lyon conurbation which is only 70km (43 miles) away while, in the north, the Parisian market is within easy reach.

Without a doubt, wine is the principal product of Burgundy, with 28,000ha (69,000 acres) of land given over to the cultivation of grapes, mostly in the east of the region. Although this represents only one-third of the area covered by the vineyards of Bordeaux, Burgundy wine has a worldwide reputation. But it is not just quality that counts: skilful marketing has also played an important part. Of the 120 million bottles sold annually, a good half of them go to other European countries and to the USA. Grape growing is confined to a long, narrow strip which starts about 150km (90 miles) south of Paris and continues south to within 60km (37 miles) of Lyon. The five main wine-producing regions are Chablis, Côte d'Or, Chalonnais, Mâconnais and Beaujolais. Of the latter only a small section lies within Saône-et-Loire; the rest belongs to the Rhône *département*.

Agriculture, too, is very important, with most of the available land given over to arable farming. As far as livestock is concerned, the Charolais cattle are the pride of the local farmers, while the Bresse poultry, bred in the south of the region, have the rare distinction of carrying an *appellation contrôlée*. In the west, the Morvan has its own industry, mostly related to forestry, including sawmills, the production of charcoal, and quality furniture.

The 5,000 industrial concerns in Burgundy employ just under 150,000 people – about a quarter of the working population. In addition to the motor industry, electronics and the manufacture of electrical components, many firms are involved in precision engineering and metal processing. In recent decades, a number of industrial centres have undergone drastic change. The closure of coal mines in the Le Creusot region, for example, has led to serious economic decline and job losses. During the early 1990s the unemployment rate for the region varied between 11 and 12 percent, but these are official figures and they probably conceal the true number of people who have been affected by the structural changes.

Administration

The Burgundy region is divided into four administrative regions, known as *départements*. These are Côte d'Or, Saône-et-Loire, Nièvre and Yonne. These *départements* consist of 15 sub-districts (*arrondissements*), 174 *cantons* and 2,044 *communes*. The main centres of population are Dijon (pop. 230,400), Chalon-sur-Saône (pop. 54,500), Nevers (pop. 45,000), Auxerre (pop. 40,000), Mâcon (pop. 37,000) and Le Creusot (pop. 29,000).

Life in the vineyards

Charolais cattle – pride of local farmers

Historical Highlights

21000–17000BC Stone tools found at the Rock of Solutré near Mâcon prove that a settlement exisited here in prehistoric times.

52BC Caesar attacks the troops of Vercingetorix, chieftain of the Gallic Arverni tribe, near Alesia. Vercingetorix surrenders.

15BC The Romans found the settlement of Augustodunum, now Autun.

About AD275 Attacks by Alemanni and Frankish armies end the relatively peaceful period of Roman rule.

About 300 Christianity gains a foothold in the region.

AD407 East Germanic Burgundians (originally from the Baltic) cross the Rhine and settle in the Saône Valley under Roman protection.

457 The County of Burgundy, with Geneva as capital, established by King Gundioc.

474 Reign of Gundobad. Second Burgundian Empire reaches its peak.

534 Burgundy becomes part of the Frankish Merovingian empire.

737 Charles Martel defeats the invading Saracens and makes himself master of Burgundy.

9th century As the Frankish empire collapses, the kingdoms of Lower and Upper Burgundy emerge.

910 William of Aquitaine founds the Benedictine abbey at Cluny.

919–955 The region is subjected to a series of invasions by the Magyars (Hungarians). They are finally routed by the German king Otto I at the Battle of Lechfeld.

933 King Rudolf II reunites the Kingdom of Burgundy.

936 Separation of Duchy of Burgundy and Duchy of France, which includes Paris.

987 First Capetian king, Hugh Capet, ascends the throne of France.

1015 Robert Capet of France takes Burgundy.

1016 Dijon falls to the Burgundians.

1021 Robert Capet's second son, also Robert, becomes hereditary duke of Burgundy.

1098 Order of Cistercians founded at Cîteaux.

1146 St Bernard preaches the second crusade at Vézelay.

1178 Frederick Barbarossa becomes King of Burgundy.

1186 Struggle between Duke Hugh III of Burgundy and Philip Augustus of France.

1193 Holy Roman Emperor Henry VI awards the crown of Burgundy to Richard the Lionheart.

1281 The Anglo-Burgundian alliance thwarts attempts to restore peace between France and Burgundy.

1315 The French retreat from Burgundy.

1337 The English king Edward III revives his claim to the French throne, marking the beginning of the Hundred Years' War. Burgundy sides with the English.

1346 English victorious at the Battle of Crécy.

1348 Burgundy is ravaged by Black Death.

1361 With the death of Philip de Rouvres, the line of Capetian dukes in Burgundy ends.

1363 Period of rule by the four dukes of the Valois dynasty begins. Burgundy becomes an important European power.

1384 Philip the Bold inherits Flanders and the 'Free County' of Burgundy.

1419 Murder of John the Fearless, probably at the instigation of the French Dauphin.

1430 Burgundian troops capture Joan of Arc at Compiègne and hand her over to the English.

1477 Charles the Bold is killed fighting the French and Swiss near Nancy. The Burgundian empire comes to an end.

1513 Habsburg troops invade Dijon.

1562–1601 Religious wars between Catholics and Protestants devastate the region.

1602 Duchy of Burgundy annexed to France and enlarged by addition of Bresse, Bugey and Valromey.

1631–1789 Burgundy ruled by the princes of Condé.

1618–48 Burgundy is ravaged in the Thirty Years' War.

1642 Briare Canal and Rogny lock-system completed.

1648–53 Aristocratic revolt known as the Fronde, led by the Great Condé.

1750 University of Burgundy founded.

1789 Outbreak of French Revolution. Rioting in Champagne spreads to Burgundy.

1791 Division of the province of Burgundy into three *départements*: Côte d'Or, Chalon-sur-Saône and Yonne. The former *comté* (county) of Nivernais becomes the Nièvre *département*.

1814–15 The Allied nations invade Burgundy when Napoleon I rejects conditions of the Congress of Châtillon-sur-Seine.

1815 First wine auctions held at Beaune.

1834 Burgundy Canal opened.

1836 Important iron foundries established by Adolphe Schneider at Le Creusot.

1851 Paris–Dijon railway line completed.

1871 Burgundy occupied by Prussians.

1878 Phylloxera destroys the vineyards.

1934 Brotherhood of the Knights of Tastevin founded at Clos de Vougeot to promote the wines of Burgundy.

1899–1901 Strikes cripple the mining region around Le Creusot and Montceau-les-Mines.

1940–44 German occupation. The forests of the Châtillonais used as a base by French resistance fighters.

1954 Death of the French writer Colette, a native of Puisaye.

1972 Burgundy becomes one of 22 new French regions.

1983 The Paris to Lyon TGV (high-speed train) passes through Burgundy for the first time.

1985 Autun, the town founded by the Romans, celebrates its 2,000th anniversary.

The Dukes of Burgundy

Burgundy can justifiably be described as one of the oldest civilised cultures of central Europe. Between 1364 and 1477 four dukes created one of Europe's most powerful states.

The first was **Philip the Bold** (1364–1404). By marrying Margaret of Flanders in 1369, he laid the foundations for the Burgundian-Low Countries empire.

His son **John the Fearless** (1404–19) inherited the Burgundian crown at the age of 33. Like his father, he sought to overshadow the French crown and this brought him into conflict with the protectors of the mentally-ill French king Charles VI. In 1407 John had his main rival, Louis d'Orléans, murdered, but was then murdered himself.

In alliance with the English, John's son **Philip the Good** (1419–67) continued to oppose the French. For a short time under his rule Burgundy was a politically autonomous state and a leading European power.

The last of the great dukes was **Charles the Bold** (1467–77). When he tried to conquer Lorraine, he was hoping to create a corridor between Burgundy's northern and southern possessions, but near Nancy in 1477 he was opposed by the combined forces of Louis XI, the Swiss confederates and the Duke of Lorraine. Charles met his death in this battle, bringing an end to the Burgundian empire.

Place de la Libération, Dijon
Preceding pages:
Semur-en-Auxois

Port Guillaume

Route 1:

★★★ Dijon – Treasure of the dukes of Burgundy

With its network of narrow cobbled streets, the old town of Dijon resembles a medieval cobweb. The splendid facades which hide what were once the residences of wealthy families, parliamentary presidents and religious dignitaries serve as a reminder that Dijon once lay at the heart of a proud and prosperous empire. But wars of religion once raged here too, around the ageing half-timbered cottages with flaking plaster. On a bright summer morning, as the shouts of the market traders echo down the alleys, it is easy to imagine that a glorious past lurks in practically every corner of this ancient town.

History

Many regional capitals in France can look back over centuries of steady growth. Not Dijon. In Gallo-Roman times, this settlement on the banks of the Ouche was an insignificant market town, nothing more than a staging post on the Via Agrippina, the Roman road that linked Lyon with Trier. In the 3rd century AD the city fathers built a wall around Castrum Divio as a defence against marauding Germanic tribes. At about the same time, a religious cult was developing at the grave of the martyr Benignus and the site of his last remains became a place of pilgrimage. After the saint appeared in a vision before the bishop of Langres, the town's secular and spiritual leader at the time, the church abandoned its disapproving stance towards the Benignus cult and in 535 a Benedictine abbey was built outside the town on the site of his grave.

The rule of the bishop of Langres ended in 1016, when Robert II bought the town and incorporated it into the duchy of Burgundy. In 1137 a fire destroyed the town and hardly a house remained. A grander town emerged from the charred ruins, but Dijon continued to be a small provincial centre. Fortunes changed dramatically in 1363, when the first ambitious duke of the Valois dynasty put Dijon at the heart of a powerful new empire. Philip the Bold, successor to the now defunct Capetian dynasty, transformed Burgundy into one of the most important territories in medieval Europe.

With the death in 1477 of the last duke, Charles the Bold, not only did the Burgundian empire come to an end, but Dijon also lost its fame and influence as a cultural centre. Not until the 18th century did the town's star begin to wax again. Dijon became the residence for a bishop and then the nobility and wealthy citizens chose to build marvellous palaces for themselves here. Many of these buildings remain and their dignified facades overlook the squares and streets in the heart of the city. During the 19th century Dijon grew into an important commercial base through its strategically important location at the hub of waterways and then railways. More recently, the motorway network and the new high-speed trains have contributed to the city's commercial advancement. While the region has gained in importance as an industrial centre, it continues to be associated in many people's minds more with the production of fine wines and mustard than with coal mining and textiles.

Rue Verrerie

City tour

At the heart of Dijon lies the semi-circular **Place de la Libération**, a vast open space surrounded by columns in classical style which dates from the end of the 17th century. It was the work of Jules Hardouin-Mansart, the man responsible for Versailles, the magnificent palace near Paris that was built for Louis XIV. This brilliant court architect would probably turn in his grave if he knew that his grand square was being used as a car park.

On the other side of the **Rue de la Liberté** the huge ★ **Palais des Ducs et des Etats de Bourgogne** ❶ with its broad facade and two wings overlooks the Cour d'Honneur courtyard. A Roman castle originally occupied this site, but between 1450 and 1455 the plain **Tour Philippe-le-Bon** was built on its foundations (Easter to end of November daily 9am–noon and 2.30–5.30pm, closed Monday afternoon, Saturday and Sunday). The view from the top of the 50-m (165-ft) high tower extends across the rooftops of the old town and it is easy to see why Dijon is sometimes called the 'city of a hundred bell-towers'. The **Tour de Bar**, where the Duke of Bar was incarcerated for four years, dates from 100 years before the Tour Philippe-le-Bon, but most of the palace was added much later. The

Tour Philippe-le-Bon: a gargoyle's view

Cour de Bar

Musée des Beaux-Arts

west wing, for example, dates from the 17th century. The French king stayed in the palace when he visited Burgundy and, by then, Dijon had become the headquarters of the 'States', a regional assembly of the nobility, clergy and deputies who all required space to hold meetings and to fulfil their administrative duties.

Today the palace serves as Dijon's town hall. Two passageways lead from the front courtyard into the inner courtyards of the two wings. The **Cour de Flore** on the left side is surrounded mainly by municipal offices, but the right courtyard, the **Cour de Bar**, is overlooked by the Musée des Beaux-Arts. Near the Tour de Bar, a staircase in Renaissance style leads up to the museum's **Galerie de Bellegarde**.

The priceless treasures of the ★★ **Musée des Beaux-Arts** (Museum of Fine Arts) are exhibited in several wings of the palace (Monday, Wednesday to Saturday, 10am–6pm, Sunday and public holidays 10am–12.30pm and 2–6pm; hour-long guided tours in English). The collection of works of art, which includes sculptures, carvings, gold and enamel, drawings and paintings range from classical antiquity to recent times. Artists from Italy, the Netherlands, Switzerland and Germany are represented here. Famous names such as Rogier van der Weyden, Melchior Broederlam, Jean de Marville and Claus Sluter worked for the dukes of Burgundy at the end of the 14th and beginning of the 15th century and examples of their paintings and sculptures are among the highlights in this, one of the finest art museums in France.

On the ground floor, in addition to the former chapterhouse and an exhibition devoted to the history of the ducal palace, the 15th-century kitchens may be viewed. A

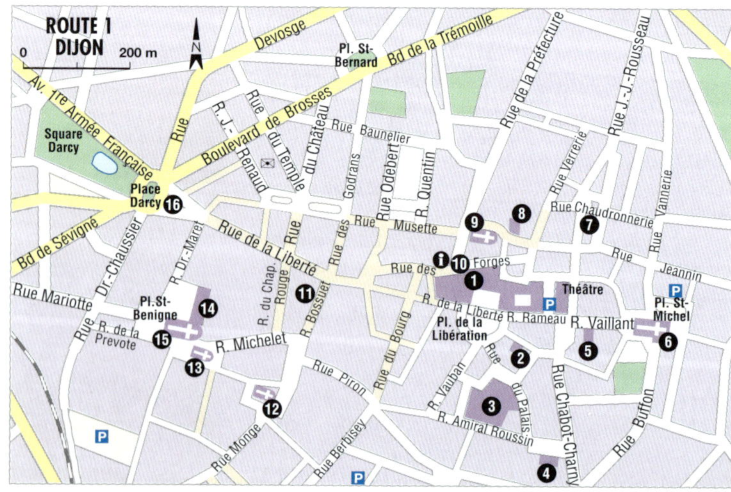

team of hand-picked cooks required six huge chimneys to cook the oxen and wild boar, pheasants and joints of lamb for the ducal banquets. It is now only a bare room, so the frenzied atmosphere as the chefs prepared for dinner amid the steaming soup terrines and spits of sizzling meat can only be imagined.

Waiting on the first floor is a fine array of masterpieces of European painting, sculpture and wood carving that date from the 14th to the 19th centuries. However, it is the famous ★★ **Salle des Gardes**, the old banqueting hall, which was built during Philip the Good's years, that deserves most attention.

Since the early 19th century, this long, narrow room has been the home for two magnificent tombs, which serve as monuments to the splendour of the Burgundian empire and its protagonists, the Valois dynasty. Back in the 14th century, Philip the Bold had decided to break with the tradition of his Capetian predecessors who had all been buried at Cîteaux. He wanted to be laid to rest closer to his people in Dijon, so he commissioned architects and artists to design somewhere suitably royal and dignified for himself and his successors. Sadly, little remains of the Chartreuse de Champmol, the original home of the Burgundian dukes' tombs. The site now lies within the grounds of a psychiatric hospital. It was destroyed during the French Revolution and today all that can be seen are the portal of the monastery church, a staircase and the so-called Well of Moses, a massive calvary with statues of Moses and the prophets, thought to be the work of the master sculptor Claus Sluter. For many, the French Revolution meant a break with the past. Kings and dukes represented feudalism and any symbols of their existence were vandalised.

Having been faithfully restored, the original tombs were transferred to the Salle des Gardes in 1827. The black marble slab of Philip the Bold's sarcophagus – he died suddenly in 1404 – is borne by a funeral procession of 40 statuettes known as the *pleurants* (the weepers). This moving work was probably started by Claus Sluter and then finished by his nephew Claus de Werve. On top of the polished plate lies an alabaster replica of the duke. His head is flanked by two angels, creating a truly princely monument to ducal splendour and Burgundian grandeur.

The second tomb in the Salle des Gardes contains the remains of John the Fearless and his wife Margaret of Bavaria. Like Philip the Bold's tomb, it took decades to finish. After the duke was murdered in 1419, Claus de Werve started work on a design that was completed by the sculptors Jean de Huerta and Antoine Le Moiturier. In the same room stands an ensemble of two gilded altarpieces. They were carved by Jacques de Baerze at the end of the 14th century for the Chartreuse de Champmol.

Sculpture is on the first floor

19

Salle des Gardes: final resting place for dukes

Inside the Musée Magnin

Just a few yards away from the palace, the **Musée Magnin** ❷ (4 rue des Bons Enfants) contains over 2,000 paintings, drawings and *objets d'art* by European artists spanning a period of 400 years. That this building is a museum is not obvious from the outside. Formerly a private house, it has retained much of its original character.

Jeanne and Maurice Magnin bequeathed their private collection to the French government in 1937. Their intention was to acquire works of art representative of Dutch, Italian and French painting between the 16th and 19th centuries, rather than works by famous artists.

Palais de Justice

The **Palais de Justice** ❸ with its splendid Renaissance gable dates from 1572. Situated in the **Rue du Palais**, it was formerly the meeting-place of the Burgundian parliament. In the days before the French Revolution, it was used as the Supreme Court and the peaceful atmosphere which existed then in the vast 40-m (130-ft) long lobby or **Salle de Pas Perdus** with its impressive barrel-vaulted ceiling prevails there today. The public are not allowed access when the courts are sitting. At the end of the lobby is the entrance to the **Chambre Dorée** with its gilded coffered vaulting. The chamber of the civil courts and also the chapel designed by the Renaissance artist Hugues Sambin is decorated with some fine carvings. This celebrated sculptor was also responsible for the entrance doors to the Palais de Justice, although these are only replicas. The originals are in the Musée des Beaux-Arts.

The reading room of the **Bibliothèque municipale** ❹ (5 rue de l'Ecole de Droit) was formerly the Renaissance chapel of the old Jesuit college. As well as more than 300,000 volumes, the library also possesses a number of extremely rare illuminated manuscripts from the Abbey of Cîteaux (*see page 27*), one of which dates from the first half of the 12th century.

The **Musée Rude** ➎ celebrates the life and work of the Dijon-born sculptor François Rude (1784–1855). The former cathedral of St-Etienne in which the museum is housed is also used by the local Chamber of Commerce. Most of the works on display are casts of Rude's better-known sculptures, including the famous relief called *Le Départ* which he created for the Arc de Triomphe in Paris. In many of his works it is still possible to detect elements of the classical training which he received at Dijon's School of Drawing.

Musée Rude: Le Départ

The church of **St-Michel** ➏ with its two domed towers and huge facade is situated in the square of the same name and is an important Dijon landmark. When work started on the foundations for the nave and the three round-arched portals at the end of the 15th century, the plans that had been drawn up were for a late Gothic structure, but the influence of the 16th-century Renaissance style is evident throughout the rest of the building. The delightful exterior is no match for the plain and gloomy interior.

Rue Vannerie with its mixture of half-timbered houses and dignified mansions leads off **Place St-Michel**, marking the beginning of the picturesque old quarter. **Rue Chaudronnerie** which winds through the old town is a tribute to the city's Renaissance architects. **Maison des Cariatides** ➐ with its 12 caryatids decorating the facade is probably the best example. Broad shoulders and arms support the window balconies, window ledges and upper stories. More treasures of the old town are only visible to walkers in Rue Verrerie. Concealed decorative work, carved figures and plinths chiselled out of grey stone are the supports for the centuries-old crooked and weathered wooden beams.

Perhaps not quite so impressive, but nevertheless typical of the town's old houses, is the **Hôtel de Vogüé** ➑ on **Rue de la Chouette**. It was built by Hugues Sambin in 1614 as a grand town house for the first president of the Burgundian parliament, Etienne Bouhier. Sculptures by Sambin adorn the inner courtyard. To the left is the **Maison Millière**, which was built in the 15th century. The marvellous half-timbered facade leans trustingly over the arcade windows of the ground floor towards the adjacent ★★ **Notre-Dame** church ➒, so that only a narrow passage separates the two buildings.

Hôtel de Vogüé

This tall church was built in the first half of the 13th century and ranks as one of the finest Gothic structures in Burgundy. As daylight fades over the roofs of the city, the sun's rays pick out the west front and its tiers of gargoyles, transforming the yellowish limestone blocks into pure gold. Viewed from the ancient Rue Musette, this building then reveals its true architectural splendour. Above the tall pointed arches at ground-floor level rises

Notre-Dame

21

Notre-Dame: the choir

the compact facade, which is broken up only by delicate arcades. Two graceful bell-turrets crown the towers. A tale is told about the clock at the top of the right-hand tower. At the end of the 14th century, Philip the Bold marched to Flanders with his army to put down a revolt in the Flemish city of Courtrai. As prize booty, his soldiers brought back to Dijon Courtrai's clock-tower. In 1610 the people of Dijon felt that the hammer, nicknamed Jacquemart, needed a female companion. Two children followed in 1714 and 1881.

While Notre-Dame has an unusual external appearance, the harmony and lightness of its triple-naved interior make a striking contrast. The Black Madonna in the right-hand apse has been the object of veneration since the 16th century. Art historians reckon it to be one of the oldest wooden madonnas in France. The people of Dijon believe she has special powers, having saved the town twice: once in 1513 when the Swiss besieged the town and again in 1944 when it was liberated from the Nazis.

The north front is a place for the superstitious. Many locals have faith not only in the Black Madonna but also in Dijon's most famous talisman: set into one of the pillars is a fist-sized stone owl which should only be touched by those in search of wisdom and happiness. The poor bird has been handled so much that it is almost impossible to recognise.

The old residences in **Rue des Forges** ought to be part of an architectural town trail. These houses accurately reflect the economic prosperity that followed from Burgundy's acquisition of Flanders and the expansion of the tightly-controlled state as far as the North Sea. That was where trade and the cloth industry really flourished and, ultimately, bankers, merchants and officials all profited. They had grand town houses built and then furnished them in a way which showed off their wealth and influence.

Dijon's most famous talisman
Rue des Forges

The late Gothic **Hôtel Chambellan** is a good example of the favoured architectural style of the time. It now houses the *Syndicat d'Initiative,* one of Dijon's tourist offices (34 rue des Forges). The premises once belonged to a wealthy cloth merchant, who combined money with power and was the town's mayor for a time. It is well worth making a detour to view the magnificent inner courtyard with its pergolas and grand spiral staircase. Other houses, such as **Hôtel Milsand** (No 38), are noted for their Renaissance facades. The **Hôtel Aubriot** (No 40) dates from the 13th century and was once the residence of the town's first banker. It possesses a portal, adorned with statues, beneath a roof of colourfully-glazed tiles, while the **Hôtel Morel-Sauvegrain** (No 56) has a 15th-century facade. Rue des Forges underlines Dijon's claim to have, after Paris, the finest town houses in the whole of France.

In **Rue Musette**, probably the oldest street in the town, **Rue des Forges** and the busy shopping street **Rue de la Liberté** a number of shops specialise in selling Dijon's best-known food products: mustard and gingerbread. *Moutarde de Dijon* is, of course, a popular brand. Look out for Grey-Poupon's company shop in **Rue de la Liberté**. A superb range of hand-painted porcelain mustard pots are on display in the window. Anyone wishing to learn more about the history of mustard should pay a visit to the **Musée de la Moutarde**, run by the AMORA company (quai Nicolas-Rolin, tel: 80 44 44 52). In the 17th century local people bought gingerbread from street traders, but now it can be obtained from confectioners under the name *pain d'épices.*

Place François-Rude ❿ is a delightful square, particularly in the summer. It is situated in a pedestrian precinct away from the traffic. Surrounded by a number of half-timbered buildings, the square has as its centrepiece a fountain with a statue of a *bareuzai*, a dialect term for a bare-footed grape-treader. This sculpture, finished in 1904, was created by François Rude, one of Dijon's most famous sons. During the first week of September, the square and surrounding area are full to bursting point with visitors attending the wine festival. The market stalls do not just sell the local wines but other regional produce.

On any shopping day, **Rue de la Liberté**, a happy mix of department stores and smaller shops, will be as busy as Place François-Rude during the wine festival. The corner of Rue de la Liberté and **Rue de Godrans** is known to the locals as **Coin du Miroir** ⓫. 'Mirror corner' is named after a building which no longer exists, but clearly it offered a good view of the parades and processions which passed down Rue de la Liberté.

The Gothic church of **St-Jean** ⓬ in Place Bossuet, badly damaged during the French Revolution, was partly

Hôtel Aubriot, details

Moutarde de Dijon

*Manuscript in the
Musée Archéologique*

Cathédrale St-Bénigne

The Romanesque crypt

demolished during the 19th century. It is now used as a stage by a theatre company. The square itself is named after Jacques-Bénigne Bossuet (1627–1704), who made a name for himself as a preacher after training at a Jesuit college at the court of Louis XIV. Many of the elegant houses around the square were built for members of the Burgundian parliament.

Begun in the 12th century but not finished until the 15th, the church of **St-Philibert** ❸ in **Rue Danton** is the only surviving Romanesque religious building in Dijon. It is soon to become part of the **Musée Archéologique** ❹ in **Rue Docteur-Maret** (No 7). Most of this museum is housed in buildings belonging to the Benedictine monastery of St-Bénigne. The locally-found artefacts and works of art displayed here date from ancient, Roman and medieval times.

Historically speaking, the centre of Dijon has always been the ★★ **Cathédrale St-Bénigne** ❺ which stands in the square of the same name. It dates from the last quarter of the 13th century and was constructed on the site of Guglielmo da Volpiano's older church which marked the spot where St Benignus was buried. This 3rd-century saint – one of the most important Christian missionaries to work in the region – fled from persecution in Lyon and was later martyred. During the 19th century, the saint's sarcophagus was discovered and it now stands in the cathedral's Romanesque crypt.

The present structure was built after the crossing tower of its five-naved predecessor collapsed in 1272. Before the completion of the abbey at Cluny (*see page 64*), the basilica at St-Bénigne must have been one of the largest religious buildings in Christendom. The new Gothic church, which was consecrated in 1394, incorporated the old west portal and a three-storey early Romanesque rotunda that was demolished during the French Revolution. Several other parts of the building as well as precious fixtures also fell victim to revolutionary fervour and much of the 19th century was taken up with the restoration of the building after the upheavals of 1789. Many of the pieces of sculpture and tombstones that are now on view inside the church come from other sacred buildings.

Porte Guillaume ❻, a monumental triumphal arch, separates **Rue de la Liberté** from the busy **Place Darcy** where the Office du Tourisme is situated. In a park at the western end of the square, water from a stone shell splashes into the basin of a fountain. This was built in honour of the engineer, Darcy, who brought drinking water to Dijon in the late 1830s. An imposing statue of a polar bear stands at the eastern entrance to this park which, in summer, serves as a refuge from the noise of the traffic and as a place to relax after a tiring sightseeing tour.

The park at Place Darcy

Route 2

A Burgundian hors d'oeuvre

Tour around Dijon (202km/125 miles)

With its reputation for fine wines, Côte d'Or to the south of Dijon (*see pages 34–40*) is the most famous of Burgundy's *départements*. But to the north and east of of the city, visitors will search in vain for vineyards. By the banks of the Saône there is not a vine in sight; in autumn, the air is filled with the smell of burning potato waste and cabbage waiting for the first frosts, rather than old wooden barrels. Instead of sampling local wine in gloomy cellars, travellers visit old forts that once protected Burgundy from the Habsburg-controlled Franche-Comté.

The little town of **Til-Châtel** (pop. 800) has guarded the confluence of the Ignon and Tille since Gallo-Roman times. The peaceful landscape must have been attractive to the people of that time as archaeologists have stumbled on old burial grounds, traces of human settlements and the remains of a Roman aqueduct. A Romanesque portal forms the entrance to the **Eglise St-Florent** which boasts a 9th-century font and unusually-decorated capitals. The altar – about 800 years old – rests on a stone block where St Florian is said to have been beheaded.

The Sâone near Pontailler

Eglise St-Florent at Til-Châtel

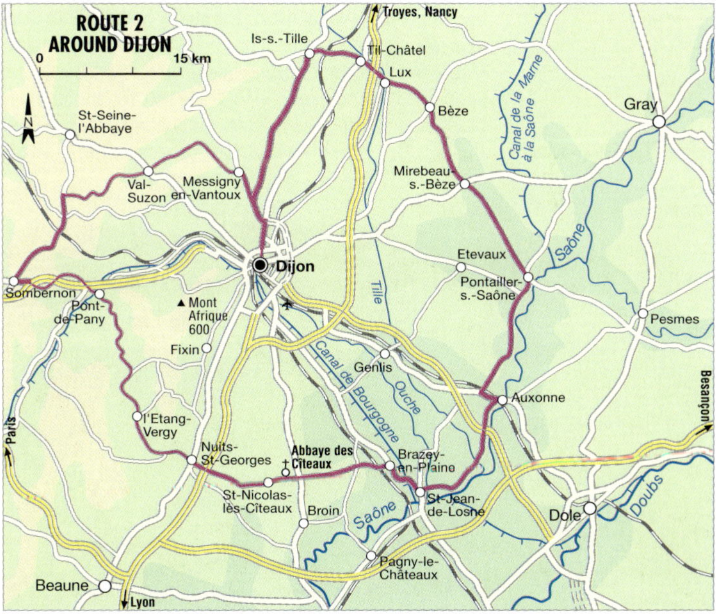

25

Notre-Dame in Auxonne

Napoleon remembered

26

As the name indicates, the existence of **Pontailler-sur-Saône** stems from its function as a bridging point (French *pont* = bridge) and two bridges still remain. It is a sleepy little place with willows overhanging the river, old river barges creaking gently against each other and the occasional fisherman trying to hook a zander.

Auxonne (pop. 7,900) was originally an important bastion on the eastern edge of Burgundy by the border with Franche-Comté, formerly a part of the Habsburg empire. Those arriving in the region from the east will find the first example of Burgundian architecture in the church of **Notre-Dame** on Place d'Armes. The church's open porch with its figurine decorations dates from the 15th century.

Napoleon stands on a plinth near the church. He came to the town in 1788 as an 18-year-old and completed a course at the artillery school during the following year. The school – built between 1759 and 1763 from pink Jura stone – is known as the **Quartier Bonaparte** (Rue du 8e Chasseurs). Apparently, the young Corsican stayed in the **château** on the banks of the Saône, and a small museum in the castle is devoted to his time in the town.

A flat area of Burgundy lies to the south of Auxonne and again there is not a vineyard in sight. Salad vegetables and cabbages are a common sight in the fields bordering the road which periodically follows the Saône.

St-Jean-de-Losne lies closer to the river than Auxonne, but it shares a place in history with the latter having also been a border town between Burgundy and the Holy Roman Empire. Two artificial waterways, the **Rhine-Rhône Canal** and the **Canal de Bourgogne** merge with the Saône here. The **Marne Canal** also flows nearby, so the town has become an important centre for boating holidays. The **Pardon des Mariniers**, a river procession of flower-

River boats at St-Jean-de-Losne

decked boats and barges, takes place in July, and hundreds of craft from rowing boats to luxury yachts and hefty cargo vessels are moored in the **Port de Plaisance**.

Together with Cluny (*see page 64–5*), the ★★ **Abbaye des Cîteaux** played an important role in the spiritual and religious life of the region. Objecting to the luxury and slack discipline of Cluny, Robert de Molesme and a number of his followers founded this Cistercian monastery in 1098. During the 12th century Bernard de Clairvaux, an important figure in the reform movement, moved to Cîteaux when it was going through a difficult period and managed to reverse its fortunes. After three years Bernard moved on again, this time to Clairvaux in the Champagne region. This monastery came to play a leading part within the Cistercian order and Bernard later took its name.

Abbaye des Cîteaux

Very little remains of the old monastery. In 1760 large parts of it were demolished and 30 years later the abbey was suppressed. At the end of thc 19th century, the monks with the white habits returned and Cîteaux regained its position at the head of the order. Now the monks live from their labours in the fields in accordance with their vow of poverty, obedience and abstinence. During the Middle Ages, the Cistercian monks were noted as much for their agricultural expertise as for their spartan lifestyle, which Bernard de Clairvaux took to such extremes that his own health suffered.

At **Nuits-St-Georges** to the south of Dijon, the itinerary crosses the *Route des Grands Crus* (*see page 38*) and those in a hurry can return north to Dijon. The D25/D35 winds up the gently-sloping hillsides of the **Haute Côte**, a longish upland limestone range of woodland, meadows and rural settlements. The Burgundian poet Lamartine once described this distinctly provincial region as the 'French Siberia' – but overworked city dwellers now regard this dismissal as more of an invitation.

Through the Haute Côte

Rather resembling a ruined castle recaptured by nature, the 600-m (1,950-ft) high **Mont Afrique** dominates the countryside to the west of Dijon. In the summer, a profusion of bright poppies carpets its slopes, contrasting delightfully with the golden brown of the cornfields. Hundreds of years ago, man must have recognised the strategic importance of this hill as Iron Age remains and pre-Christian coins have been found on the hillsides.

Welcome refreshment

The country road runs parallel to the busy A38 motorway for 5km (3 miles) from **Pont de Panny** to **Sombernon**. Branch off to the right here towards the delightfully rural landscapes of **Val-Suzon**. Dense woodland with moss-covered tree trunks lies beside the course of the

Delights of Val-Suzon

Suzon, which in its upper reaches can hardly be called a river. The area resembles a nature reserve in which the road itself is the only sign of human intervention. Halfway to Val-Suzon, wooden picnic tables placed beneath shady trees make an inviting place to stop. On summer weekends several car parks encourage ramblers to abandon four wheels in favour of walking shoes.

Val-Suzon consists of two parts. The river of the same name meanders through the widening valley and marshy pasture. Gleaming limestone rocks stand out like weathered castle ruins at several spots on the edge of wooded hill slopes. The comparison is actually not that unrealistic as it seems certain that both sides of the Suzon Valley were used by prehistoric man. Archaeologists have found evidence of settlements dating from the middle of the Late Stone Age, i.e. about 5,000 years ago. Finds such as millstones and various tools from the 2,000 years before the birth of Christ indicate the existence of a pastoral culture, similar to ones found in other parts of Burgundy. Fortified settlements on the sides of the valley such as **Châtelet d'Etaules** and **Châtelet de la Fontaine-au-Chat** are thought to date from that time, but they can only be reached on foot. Although the sites of these settlements were chosen for the protection they offered, the oldest fortifications dating from about 800BC still took the form of ramparts made from limestone slabs.

If stomachs are rumbling and legs are tired from so much walking – or night is falling – the **Hostellerie du Val-Suzon** (Val-Suzon, RN71) surrounded by a beautiful flower garden, is ideal for a break or overnight stop. The rural charm of both the restaurant and accommodation is typical of this unspoilt country area.

Route 2 finishes in **Messigny-en-Vantoux**, a village noted for its 18th-century castle known as **Vantoux-les-Dijon**. Dijon is only 10km (7 miles) to the south.

Hostellerie du Val-Suzon

Route 3

★★ Beaune – A paradise for lovers of good wine

Beaune town centre is the place to be on a Saturday morning. Farmers from the outlying villages arrive, their vans laden with tomatoes, onions, leeks and potatoes. At the *charcuterie* stalls, traders set out their thick sausages and pink hams while, in the covered hall, the counters are overflowing with cheeses: round and long, thick and thin, yellow and white. Discerning customers stand and stare, sniff and nibble, drift from stall to stall. Nowhere else in France is the choice of produce so rich and varied.

Beaune market

History

Even before the town was discovered by tourists, Beaune (pop. 21,200) played a more important part in the region's economy than Dijon. This was due not to its historical significance but rather to its vineyards. Since the 18th century, Beaune has been the Burgundian capital of the trade in what Louis Pasteur called the 'healthiest and safest of all drinks'. But the fermented grape juice has been an important factor in the life of the townsfolk for much longer than that. Even in Roman times, the city prospered as a major centre of viticulture.

Viticulture goes back a long way

In pre-Christian times, the Celts worshipped the god of light, Belen or Belenos, at a sacred site near the sources of the Bouzaise and Aigue rivers. Over the centuries the name for the settlement changed to Beaune. During those early years, the market town attracted little attention, but it expanded and by the 12th century it was felt necessary to build a wall around the town. In 1227, the first Burgundian Parliament met at Beaune, and the city subsequently became the residence of the dukes of Burgundy. The fact that the dukes of the Valois dynasty later moved their residence to Dijon is still a source of animosity between the two towns.

When the Hundred Years' War ended in the middle of the 15th century, Beaune suffered badly from attacks and sackings by marauding soldiers. That may be the reason why Philip the Good's chancellor, Nicholas Rolin, decided to build what is now the Hôtel-Dieu, a hospital for the poor, in Beaune rather than in his home town of Autun. The trustees of this splendid building, one of the finest sights in the whole region, own large vineyards and they auction off their wines at an annual festival in November.

Town tour

The old town with its medieval palace, narrow lanes, little squares and quiet courtyards has survived the past few centuries almost unscathed. It lies within the confines of

The Hôtel-Dieu

medieval ramparts and bastions and then, beyond that, at a respectable distance, it is encircled by a broad ring road. Parts of the 15th-century wall, now overgrown with bushes and wild cherries, remain. It protects the old town from the advances of the motor-car and the wine warehouses which lie concealed beneath it.

For visitors, **Place de la Halle** ❶ is the centre of the town. The famous Saturday market is held inside and in front of the hall. In summer, there are so many stalls that they overflow into nearby **Place Carnot**.

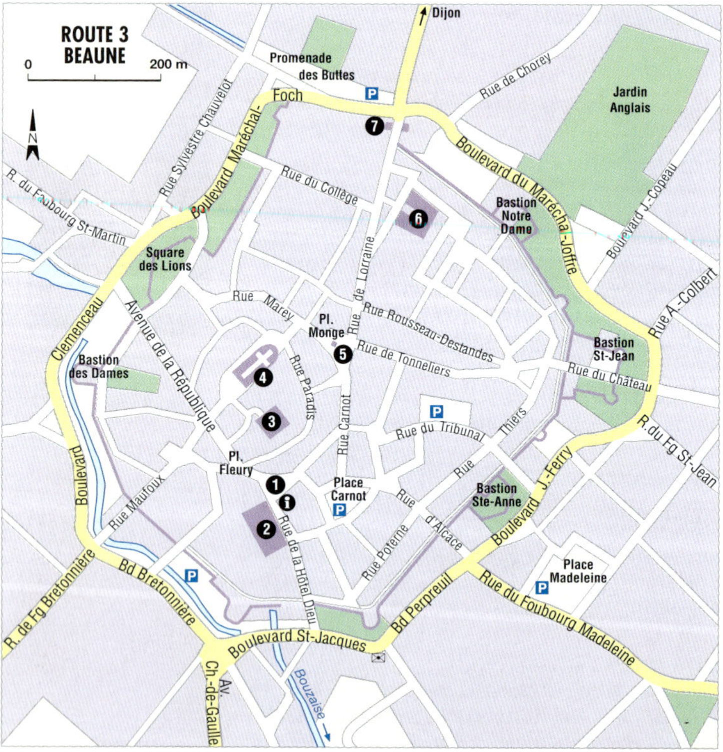

Tourists, almost without exception, head straight for the ★★ **Hôtel-Dieu** ❷, by far the most outstanding building in the town (March to mid-November 9am–6.30pm, otherwise daily 9–11.30am and 2–5.40pm). After the plain exterior, the splendour within this Burgundian-Flemish style hospital surprises many visitors. A long, half-timbered balcony resting on slim columns overlooks the inner courtyard and octagonal well. Photographs of the Hôtel-Dieu always dwell on the steep dormer windows with their weather vanes and on the roof with its yellow, black, green and ochre glazed tiles arranged in geometric patterns. However it needs to be said that, although the hospital itself dates from the 15th century, the patterned roof decoration was added early this century and it is inside where the real treasures lie. The huge **Salle des Pauvres**, (50 by 14m/165 by 45ft) has a magnificent timber roof in the shape of an upturned boat and the 28 beds – this ward was in use until 1971 – are arranged along the long wall in nautical style with each 'bunk' draped with red curtains. Each one was intended to accommodate two patients.

At the end of the tiled room, a carved screen separates the ward from the **chapel**. A nine-panel polyptych, which once stood on the altarpiece and showed the Last Judgement, was the work of Rogier van der Weyden (1400–64). It survived the French Revolution, as it was hidden well away from the bands of marauding vandals, but now needs to be kept in a special air-conditioned room. At the centre, Christ, wrapped in a gleaming red robe, sits on a rainbow. His feet rest on a globe, while beneath, St Michael, flanked by trumpeting angels, weighs two naked souls on scales. The outer panels immortalise the founder of the hospital Nicholas Rolin (1376–1462) and his wife Guigone de Salins. Rolin earned his fortune, said to have been of legendary proportions, by rather unscrupulous means. He was a legal adviser and diplomat in the court of John the Fearless and then chancellor under his successor Philip the Good. Historians ascribe his generosity in founding the hospital less to his concern for the poor and underprivileged and more to the practice at that time of making donations for the good of the community in order to secure a place in heaven. Rolin's utterances leave us in no doubt that this was intention: 'By this sacred act I wish to exchange the earthly, that was granted me by the grace of God, for the heavenly'.

Beaune's hospital, to which the Hôtel-Dieu belongs, still profits from Rolin's generosity. As well as woods and meadows, the hospital also owns 58ha (143 acres) of vineyards. A dozen or so farmers tend the vines and, when the annual yield is auctioned every November, the hospital benefits to the tune of several million francs.

How the Hôtel-Dieu functioned on a day-to-day basis can be seen in the **kitchen** where copper kettles hang by the huge fireplace alongside polished jugs and bowls and in the apothecary where original equipment such as mortars, pans and earthenware are displayed. The kitchen was brought back into use for a time during World War II.

The **ducal residence** is hidden away in a narrow lane known as Rue d'Enfer or Street of Hell. The restored building which consists of a stair tower and half-timbered galleries overlooks an irregularly-shaped courtyard. In some respects it is a smaller version of the Hôtel-Dieu. This was where the dukes lived when they came to preside over sessions of the Burgundian parliament or moved their court

Salle des Pauvres

31

Kitchen utensils

Musée du Vin de Bourgogne

Inside Notre-Dame

The Beffroi on Place Monge

to Beaune in the autumn to keep an eye on the wine harvest. The premises are now used to house the ★★ **Musée du Vin de Bourgogne** ❸ (daily 9.30am–6pm; 21 November to 31 March closed Tuesday afternoon). A tour of the museum will reveal the development of Burgundian wine production over the centuries. Huge wooden grape presses and vats stand in one of cellars as reminders of a time now long gone. Other exhibits include tools, which were the forerunners of those still in use today, while the walls in one room used for official functions is decorated with splendid Gobelins tapestries.

A few steps away in **Place Général-Leclerc** stands the porch of **Notre-Dame** ❹. It was from this spot in 1443 that Nicolas Rolin publicly announced his plans for the Hôtel-Dieu. The original facade was once richly decorated with statues but, as was the case in many other French churches, these were destroyed during the Revolution.

Work started on this collegiate church around 1120 and the ground plan is very similar to that of the abbey church at Cluny (III). It took 500 years to complete so there is evidence of a wide variety of stylistic elements. The original crossing tower was destroyed by fire and was rebuilt in Renaissance style. Barrel vaulting covers the central nave, while the side aisles open into chapels which are later additions. In the right-hand aisle, the **Chapelle de Bouton** with its Renaissance-style coffered ceiling, dates from the 16th century. The five tapestries in the choir are priceless. Made from wool and silk during the 15th and 16th centuries, they originated in Flanders. It was Jean Rolin, the son of the founder and the cardinal of Autun, who commissioned the five panels which tell the story of the Virgin Mary.

The **Beffroi** ❺ on the busy Place Monge marks the geographical centre of the old town. This clock-tower was originally part of a 14th-century church. The square itself is named after a native of Beaune, the mathematician Gaspard Monge (1746–1818), who is best known as one of the earliest researchers of descriptive geometry. The statue in the middle of the square was erected in his memory. Place Monge is surrounded by beautiful town houses, including the **Hôtel de la Rochepot** (No 9), with its Gothic facade. Other more recent buildings show Renaissance influences.

Take a detour down **Rue de l'Horloge** where the **Town Hall** ❻ is situated. Before the building was handed over to local officials, it was used by Ursuline nuns. Built in the 17th century around a courtyard, it is now home to two museums, the **Musée des Beaux-Arts** and the **Musée Etienne-Jules Marey**. The art museum houses a small but fine collection of Dutch and Flemish paintings from the 15th and 16th centuries. Other exhibits include works by

Marché aux Vins

more recent French artists and also artefacts that date from Gallo-Roman times. The other museum is devoted to one of Beaune's most celebrated sons. The doctor Etienne-Jules Marey was not just interested in the well-being of his patients but he also found time for his favourite pastime, cinematography.

The historic town centre ends by the **Porte St-Nicholas** ❼. This triumphal arch was built in 1760 and is named after a church which lay outside the town walls.

Not all of Beaune's treasures are out in the open air. Millions of them are hidden away from the public gaze in countless cellars and vaults. For the precious drops of Burgundy to mature, they must be stored in bottles at an even temperature. Many of these *caves* are open to the public. Some, however, may only be visited by wine connoisseurs and buyers.

Ambassade du Vin (23 rue Paradis) is open every day and welcomes guests. The first tour (in French) starts at 11am, the second (in English) at 6pm. **Marché aux Vins** (rue Nicolas-Rolin) is open daily, 9.30am–noon and 2.30–6pm. There are 40 different wines to choose from. **La Cave du Bourgogne** (28 rue Sylvestre-Chauvelot, daily 10am–7pm; October to March, Monday to Saturday 10am–noon and 2–6pm) is one of the oldest of Beaune's cellars. Smooth red and white wines can be sampled in the crypt of a 700-year-old church. At **Caves des Cordeliers**, formerly a convent (6 rue de l'Hôtel-Dieu, daily 9am–5pm; November to March 9am–noon and 2–6.30pm), three or four different wines may be sampled free of charge. **Maison Patriarche Père et Fils** (7 rue du Collège; March to December daily 9.30–11.30am and 2–5.30pm) boasts one of the largest cellars. The bottles are stored in huge racks along a 9-km (5-mile) long underground passage and the smell of the old wooden barrels and fermenting wine can be quite overpowering.

33

Wine casks in Marché aux Vins

Tasting in Caves des Cordeliers

Vineyards near Clos de Vougeot

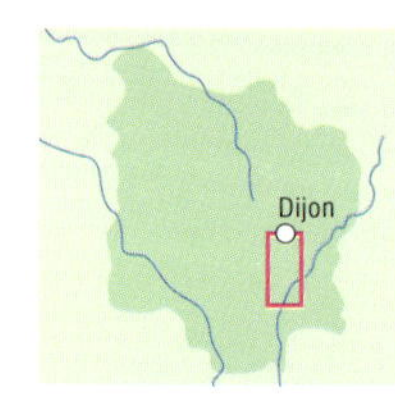

34

Famous vintages

Route 4

Through the Vineyards of Côte d'Or

The Route des Grands Crus from Dijon to Chalon-sur-Saône (160km/100 miles) *See map on pages 36–7*

Many of the grand boulevards of France are named after famous commanders and generals. There is, however, one road in Burgundy that has done more to honour the greatness of France than probably all the country's military leaders put together. The *Route des Grands Crus* passes through the Côte d'Or wine-producing region, taking in such world-famous villages as Gevrey-Chambertin, Meursault and Vougeot. The tour veers off the main road in places, passes green vineyards on the remote hillsides of the Haute Côte and stops off in tiny rural villages seemingly a million miles away from the busy motorways that criss-cross Burgundy.

Wine production in the Côte d'Or originally extended to the southern outskirts of Dijon itself, but the big city with its voracious appetite has gobbled up large parts of the vineyards of **Chenôve** and they are now occupied by rows of houses, supermarkets and an industrial zone. The **Cuverie des Ducs de Bourgogne** in the old part of Chenôve serves as a reminder of past glories. Two 13th-century grape presses are exhibited in this wine cellar that once belonged to the dukes of Burgundy. These primitive tools were used by the farmers of Fixin, the starting point for the *Route des Grands Crus*.

After Chenôve, the route follows the RN74 along the west bank of the Saône and past some of the most celebrated vineyards in the world. At the courtly festivities and ceremonies in Versailles during the reign of Louis XIV the red and white wines produced on these slopes would have been served at every table. The vines flourish on the terraced and wind-protected slopes at about 220m (700ft) above the river because of a combination of factors, but it is mainly the chalky soil, the relatively dry climate and the morning sunshine which help to produce a high sugar content in the grapes.

The dominant feature in the village of **Fixin**, where the green vines almost reach the eaves of the houses, is the brightly-patterned tiled roof of the church tower. Claude Noisot, one of Napoleon's most loyal followers, was a son of Fixin. His devotion to the Corsican was such that he commissioned from Dijon's famous sculptor, François Rude, a monument entitled *Napoleon Awakening to Immortality*. This bronze replica of the emperor can be seen in **Parc Noisot**. There is also a museum named after the officer from the Imperial Guard and it displays some Napoleon memorabilia. Wine connoisseurs, however, may choose to ignore the village's historic monuments and museum, preferring to inspect such celebrated vineyards as the **Clos du Chapitre** and **Clos de la Perrière**, which produce some of the finest Côte d'Or wines.

The statue of Napoleon ought really to have been erected in the neighbouring village of **Gevrey-Chambertin**, as the wine from here was the French emperor's favourite tipple. The vineyard, a mere 13ha (32 acres) in area, is still producing fine wines. In the mid-18th century, the community in the Côte d'Or *département* was granted special permission to add the name of its finest vineyard i.e. Chambertin to the village name. Since then, the use of the double-barrelled name has become common in the Côte de Nuits and Côte de Beaune, testifying to the commercial importance of wine production in these parts.

Topographical features, typical of the Côte d'Or, are the *combes*, gorges cut by water flowing downhill. The **Combe de Lavaux**, a deep furrow in the Haute Côte near Gevrey-Chambertin, is the northernmost of the *combes* and a car park situated 100m (110yds) from the entrance to the gorge marks the starting point for a circular walk. A path runs through the **Bois du Château Renard** into **Combe St-Martin** and then back to the car park.

Those who are interested in the scenery rather than the cultivation of grapes – albeit famous ones – could quickly tire of the *Route des Grands Crus* as the landscape varies little, apart from the occasional wrought-iron gate adorned with grape motifs or a magnificent entrance with a plate bearing the name of a top wine. So a detour into the hilly hinterland of the **Haute Côte** provides a little variation

Fixin church

Napoleon Awakening

35

A wealthy domaine

View from Abbaye de St-Vivant

without adding too much extra driving. The road winds its way past steep inclines, which receive hardly any sun, up to the hamlet of **Chamboeuf**. It is clear from the little church here that producing wine leaves little time for art, history or religion. The two dozen or so statues on plinths seem attached to the walls with cobwebs and piles of dust have accumulated on the pews.

From **Chamboeuf** the road snakes past pasture and woodland, affording a fine view across the Saône Valley. It continues via **l'Etang Vergy** and **Reulle-Vergy** to the 12th-century **Abbaye de St-Vivant**. Only a few yards from the church lies a viewpoint and the ruins of the **Château de Vergie**. A museum, **Centre des Arts et Trad-**

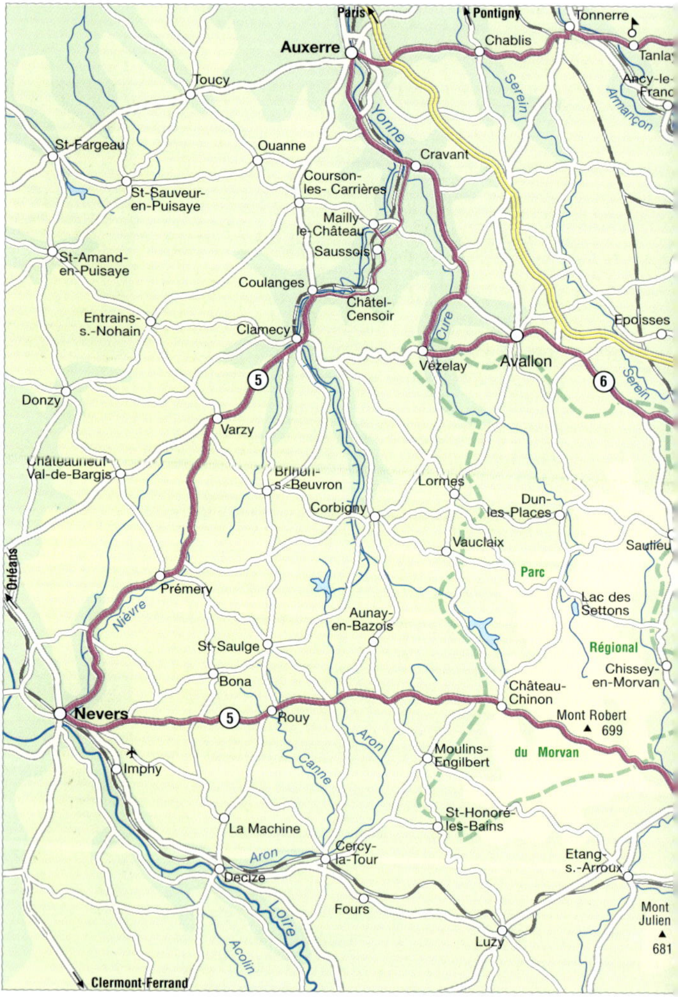

itions de Haute Côte, is devoted to the local geology, archaeology, fauna and flora, as well as the traditions and domestic architecture of the Haute Côte.

A lane runs from **Curley** through another gorge, the **Combe Ambin**, which is even wilder than the Combe de Lavaux, and then down into Vougeot on the *Route des Grands Crus*. Just before the main road lies the village of **Chambolle-Musigny** with its 16th-century church, a favourite subject for photographers. The frescoes inside date from 1539.

The most famous vineyard in the Côte de Nuits is almost certainly the **Clos de Vougeot** in **Vougeot** (1 October to

Clos de Vougeot

31 March daily 9.30am–6.30pm, 1 April to 30 September daily 9.30am–7.30pm). The *château* here rises from the expanse of vines like a grey rock from the sea. It was acquired as fallow land in the 12th century by Cistercian monks who paid two monks' habits for it. They built a monastery and planted vines outside the walls, which gradually grew into vineyards providing high yields of good wine. The 48th abbot of Cîteaux, Jean Loysier, built the Renaissance-style sections in the 16th century but, after the French Revolution, the building fell into disrepair. The *Confrérie des Chevaliers du Tastevin* (Brotherhood of the Knights of the Tastevin) eventually stepped in and reversed the building's decline. The aim of this elite organisation was declared to be the sale of good wine from the region at a competitive price, and the inaugural meeting was held in November 1934 in Nuits-St-Georges. Now, dressed in splendid red robes, these 'knights of Burgundian wine' meet in the *château* on the third Saturday in November to celebrate the start of the *Les Trois Glorieuses* (Three Glorious Days), an extravagant festival (*see page 10*).

The most impressive sections of the complex, which is built in light-coloured limestone around an inner courtyard, are the cellars dating from the *château*'s early years where ancient grape presses and fat wooden barrels can still be seen.

Tapestry in the château

Nuits-St-Georges

Nuits-St-Georges (pop. 5,500) is the main town in the **Côte de Nuits**, which extends from Fixin to Corgoloin. This delightful town with its small shops and narrow lanes should, however, be regarded more as a stopping-off point rather than a destination in its own right. It does not boast any historic castles or grand abbeys, although the 17th-century clock tower, originally part of the town hall, is of interest. The Romanesque **St-Symphorien** is also worth seeking out. Louis XIV is in some ways responsible for putting Nuits-St-Georges on the wine-lover's map. When the Sun King was suffering from a painful complaint, his physician Dr Fagon prescribed red wine from Nuits-St-Georges, recommending that a glass be taken at every meal time as a tonic. The whole royal court then developed a craving for the wine, and Madame Pompadour secretly bought the Romanée vineyard near Nuits-St-Georges, so that her lover Louis XV would stay fit and healthy.

Dedicated wine connoisseurs who wish to learn more of the secrets of Burgundian wine should make enquiries at the **Domaine Comtesse Michel de Loisy** outside Nuits-St-Georges (tel: 80 61 02 72). Guests who take full board and stay in one of the five magnificent rooms are treated to excursions to the vineyards and guided tours of the underground cellars, together with the usual tasting sessions.

The **Côte de Beaune**, Côte d'Or's southern wine region, starts at Nuits-St-Georges. Unlike many of the other villages on the *Route des Grands Crus*, in **Comblanchien** it is not the production of fine wines that pays the wages but the quarrying of salmon and ivory-coloured limestone. It is cut from the steep slopes of the Haute Côte and sold as 'Burgundian marble'.

Another detour into the hilly hinterland passes through delightful rural scenery. Head east from Comblanchien towards **Bruant** which lies at the end of the **Combe Pertuis**, before returning to the RN74 via the **Rhoin** Valley.

Aloxe-Corton has a longer wine-producing history than most of the other villages in the region. Over 1,000 years ago Charlemagne declared himself to be the owner of some of the vineyards here and these are now referred to as **Corton-Charlemagne**.

Aloxe-Corton

Follow the road south around Burgundy's wine capital of **Beaune** (*see page 29*) into **Pommard**, a name that is respected by all connoisseurs of red wine. Pommard is derived from Pomona, the Roman goddess of fruit, even though over the centuries the community has probably been more inclined to pay homage to Bacchus. The town's robust and acidic red wines were the favourites of Henri IV, Louis XV and Victor Hugo. The dukes of Burgundy frequently stopped off here – and not just to oversee the grape harvest.

The picturesque village of **Volnay** also has royal connections. Local vine growers used to supply the court of Versailles and, as a result, the French court unwittingly became an important advertising medium for Burgundian wines. The village's tree-ringed **Place de la Mairie** serves as a small viewing platform for the famous vineyards. Wine buffs will almost certainly continue south towards Meursault, another name that has a prominent place on nearly all French wine lists, but a short detour to the two pretty villages of **Monthélie** and **St-Romain** is well worth the effort. Both can boast delightful narrow alleys and hidden corners that bring charm to an otherwise monotonous landscape.

Meursault (pop. 1,600) belongs to the **Côte de Meursault** wine-producing region and is one of the few places which produces both red and white wines of high quality. Every year the farmers bottle some 15,000 hectolitres (400,000 gallons) of *premiers crus*. 'Les Gouttes d'Or', 'Les Charmes' and 'Les Perrières' are just three of Meursault's world-famous wines. The aroma and taste of the local wines inspire wine writers, with fern, flowers, caramel and burnt almonds just some of the terms used to describe the subtle flavours.

St-Romain landscape

39

Meursault

The word Meursault derives from the Latin *muris saltus* meaning 'rat's leap', a reference to the valley that divides the Côte de Meursault from the Côte de Beaune. The church of **St-Nicolas** with its 57-m (185-ft) bell-tower was modelled on the cathedral of Autun (*see Route 5, page 42*). The oldest part of the building dates from the 14th century, but the castle is probably even older. The mayor and civic officials still use the only remaining section, the huge tower. The most important date in Meursault's calendar is the third Monday in November. *La Paulée de Meursault* is the last of the three events in *Les Trois Glorieuses* (*see page 10*). The festival began as a communal banquet for the *vignerons* to mark the end of the grape harvest.

Meursault and its southern neighbours of **Puligny-Montrachet** and **Chassagne-Montrachet** are said by many to produce the top three white wines of Burgundy. The writer Alexandre Dumas remarked that these wines should only be drunk bare-headed and on bended knee.

Château de La Rochepot

The impressive **Château de La Rochepot** dominates the hamlet of **La Rochepot** like a medieval fairy-tale castle (April to May and September to November daily 10–11.30am and 2–5.30pm, June to August daily 9–11.30am and 2.30–6.30pm). Built in the 12th century, it was destroyed during the French Revolution. However, the widow of the fourth French president, Marie François Sadi Carnot (1837–94), had it rebuilt using the original plans. A diplomat and statesman by the name of Philippe Pot, who made a name for himself in London as ambassador to England for the dukes of Burgundy, was born here in 1428. The charm of the *château* lies, on the one hand, in its stunning location and on the other hand, in the whimsical interplay of its different architectural styles.

Santenay is the southernmost village in Burgundy's wine paradise. Like Comblanchien, it is not the juice of the grape that provides its lifeblood, but the lithium-rich waters which are said to work wonders on digestive disorders and rheumatism. However, large vineyards remain within sight of all the three localities that make up Santenay.

The **Hostellerie du Château de Bellecroix** (Chagny, 6 route Nationale, tel: 85 87 13 86, fax: 85 91 28 62) lies to the east of Santenay. This delightful country hotel with its ivy-covered facade and conical towers dates from the 12th century, but in the 18th century it was converted for the Order of Maltese Knights. The 21 rooms all overlook the park and each one is furnished in a different style.

Santenay, just under 20km (13 miles) from **Chalon-sur-Saône** (*see page 60*), makes a good starting point for a tour of the Mâconnais with its famous Romanesque monuments (*see pages 63–6*).

Route 5

The green heart of Burgundy

A tour through the Morvan mountains (210km/130 miles) *See map on pages 36–7*

Legends of druids, mythical figures and strange happenings abound in the green, unspoilt countryside at the heart of Burgundy, a mysterious world within easy reach of the dukes' palaces. But now that the city-dwellers have discovered its beauty, this vast wilderness, dotted with reservoirs, has become an attractive recreational area with many facilities for leisure pursuits.

The last part of the **Côte d'Or** region lies to the southwest of Beaune. Vineyards and villages occupy the gently sloping hillsides where in autumn the smell of newly-fermented grape juice permeates the narrow lanes.

The last of the *département's* vineyards is to be found on the road to **Nolay** (pop. 1,600) by the banks of the Cosanne, birthplace of the mathematician and statesman Lazare Carnot (1753–1823). In 1793 he became the French minister of war and won fame when he called for a *levée en masse*, which is to say mass conscription. A monument to this 'Organiser of Victory' stands in front of the house where he was born. The market hall with its rough-hewn chestnut beams and limestone slabs serves as a reminder of times gone by. As the farmers arrive, laden with produce, it becomes clear that the scene on market day has changed little over the years. Work on the church started in the 15th century, changes were made later and then again after a serious fire. Look closely at the shrimps set in the stone tower, which overlooks the medieval houses and tiny shops.

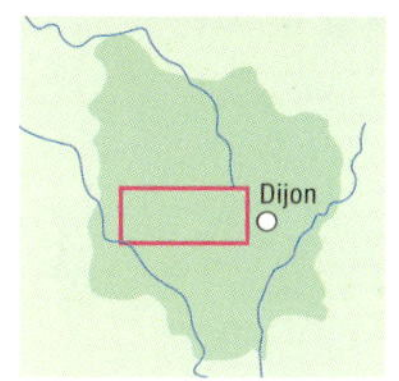
Nolay covered market

41

Nolay

Climber on the Falaises de Cormot
Château Sully

The **Falaises de Cormot** to the north of Nolay offer sporting challenges at varying degrees of difficulty. Until well into the autumn, climbers train on the difficult precipices of the **Vallée de la Tournée** at the far end of the gorge. One tributary of the Cosanne runs through the **Grotte de la Tournée**, another crashes down to the valley as an impressive waterfall. It is, however, easy to tour the area without a rope and a karabiner. Try the **Cirque du Bout du Monde** footpath from Vauchignon.

Château Sully was described by Madame de Sévigné (1626–96) in one of her letters as the Fontainebleau of Burgundy. This impressive Renaissance building with its four huge wings and corner towers encloses an inner courtyard. The fortified walls are surrounded by a moat which is fed by the River Dree and is home to scores of ducks (guided tours: mid-June to September daily 2–6pm; tours of the exterior, Easter to 1 November daily).

A glance at the map will reveal that, to the west of Sully, all roads lead to ★★ **Autun**, an important provincial town with 22,000 inhabitants. In 1995 the town celebrated 2010 years since its foundation. Even before Gaul succumbed to the Roman legions, ancient Bibracte, situated on a hill in the Arroux Valley and home of the Aedui tribe's chief, was a place where bridle paths and trade routes met. The town retained its position at the hub of this road network when the Romans established the capital of their Gallo-Roman empire here in 15BC. Renamed later as Augustodunum, it was proclaimed as Gaul's sister to Rome. In subsequent years, it was even thought of as a rival to the Imperial capital on the Tiber.

Autun has changed dramatically in the past 2,000 years, even if everyday life goes on as before. On market days (Wednesday and Friday), for example, the farmers greet

Market day in Autun

their neighbouring stall-holders with a hearty shake of the hand and a *ballon de blanc*, a well-chilled glass of white wine. Some will have wheeled their produce through the old Roman gateway of **Porte St-André** on the RN81 and **Porte d'Arroux** on the D980 on their way to market. Others will have passed along Avenue du Deuxième Dragons and the **Théâtre Romain**, Gaul's largest amphitheatre with seating for 15,000 spectators. This site was probably built around AD70. Its impressive proportions and design are easily recognised, even if generations of masons have since used the stones as a free source of building materials.

Wind and weather, war and misery have certainly taken their toll on the theatre. However, the rows of seating were restored in the 1930s and it is now used for summer festivals, highlighting Autun's continuing prominence as a religious and cultural centre. A creative spirit here has produced some astonishing achievements, including the Roman **Temple of Janus**, of which only two walls remain.

Autun's second flowering came in the first half of the 12th century with the construction of the **Cathédrale St-Lazare** in Place St-Louis, a jewel of Romanesque architecture. The townsfolk who live in the little houses around the church are now well used to seeing visitors staring up in amazement at the west portal with its ★★ **tympanum**. This fascinating picture-book, carved out of stone with simple hand tools, points out the highs and lows of human existence. Its creator, Gislebertus, used the Last Judgement as the basis for the design of the 100 figures, grouped around a central Christ figure. Chiselled out of hard limestone between 1130 and 1135, it is surely one of the finest examples of Romanesque sculpture in Burgundy. To the right of Christ, the faithful stand in a humble posture making pious gestures, while on the left, a hand from heaven weighs souls. A three-headed serpent winds itself round the legs of Satan and the damned cover their faces in horror.

But it is the richly decorated capitals that have made the cathedral famous. The finest are found in the *salle capitulaire* above the sacristy. Look out for the *Dream of the Three Kings* and the *Suicide of Judas*.

The **Musée Rolin** (25 rue des Bancs) documents the town's long history in the form of Gallo-Roman mosaics, tombstones and bronze artefacts as well as paintings and sculptures dating from the 15th century.

The **Parc Naturel Régional du Morvan** (*see also page 8–9*) which lies at the heart of Burgundy extends to the outskirts of Autun. It is a thinly populated region which has acquired a rather negative image from arrogant town dwellers and those in the more easily accessible wine-pro-

The Théâtre Romain

Concert in the cathedral

Musée Rolin: Temptation of Eve

ducing regions. One reason for their disdain probably dates from the Middle Ages as the mountains concealed both wild animals and robbers. A rather unkind saying is sometimes still heard: 'No good wind and no good people ever came out of the Morvan.'

Château-Chinon (pop. 2,600) is the unofficial centre of the Morvan and the **Musée de Septennat** (6 rue du Château) displays presents given to President Mitterrand when he came to power in 1981. Given its position in the heart of the Morvan, Château-Chinon makes a good starting point for car and walking tours. The *calvaire* (calvary) affords a fine view of the wooded landscape. This hill with its three crosses was once crowned by a Roman fort.

It is easy to understand the local people's mixed feelings towards the 'black mountain'. Away from the larger settlements, nature has gained the upper hand. Deciduous and evergreen forests line the winding roads. Hedges mark out geometric patterns on the hillsides – the trees were felled centuries ago to create grazing land for the Charolais herds. Occasionally a lonely farmstead or a hamlet consisting of no more than a handful of houses is visible by the roadside. Numerous footpaths cross these green mountains, which form an island of granite in what is predominantly a limestone region. On fine weekends, many Burgundians make their way up to the lakes, where 'a quiet life' is in no way synonymous with 'nothing to do'. On the banks of the **Lac des Settons**, for example, the camp-sites, holiday villages and restaurants are very popular, particularly during high season.

Another reason to make a detour into this part of the Morvan is to visit Burgundy's last clog-making factory at **Gouloux** (daily 9am–noon and 2–6pm). To step inside the workshop is to step back in time. No hi-tech equipment here – saws, planes and knives are still the main tools used by the craftsmen.

The Gallic Aedui tribe recognised the strategic importance of the Nièvre-Loire confluence further west. They established a settlement here and called it Noviodunum, now **Nevers** (pop. 45,000), the administrative centre for the Nièvre *département*. Seen from the old Loire bridge, the view is reminiscent of Auxerre (*see page 53*), but here it is the **Cathédrale St-Cyr-et-Ste-Juliette** which makes the first impression. Built between the 11th and 16th centuries, the basilica lacks a distinctive style, but displays instead an interesting mixture of Romanesque and Gothic elements. Evidence suggests that it was built on the foundations of a 6th-century structure. A baptismal chapel, some 1,500 years old, was found beneath a Carolingian rotunda. To be precise, the cathedral was not finished in the 16th century. Badly damaged during World War II,

44

Lac des Settons

Nevers: the cathedral and interior detail

it was extensively renovated after 1945. It is unusual in that it is one of the few churches in France which has two apses at either end of the nave.

Near the cathedral is the **Palais Ducal**, the former palace of the dukes of Nevers. This delightful complex with its elegant facade of windows, a pointed staircase tower and several corner towers was built between 1465 and 1656. It is now serves as the local law courts.

The Palais Ducal

The round corner towers and squat roof of the **Porte du Croux** probably make an even more popular subject for photographers than the Palais Ducal. The first town wall was built in the 12th century but, as the town grew in size, alterations had to be made and this huge gateway was built some 200 years later. Nevers' **Musée Archéologique du Nivernais** (Rue Porte du Croux) is now housed in the gateway and Gallo-Roman finds are among the exhibits on display here.

Stained glass in St-Etienne

St-Etienne in Rue St-Etienne enjoys a quieter existence on the edge of the town centre. For devotees of church architecture, it enjoys a higher status than the cathedral, as it is not an object lesson in the development of medieval church architecture, but pure Romanesque.

45

The route now heads northwards via **Prémery** on the Nièvre, a small country town whose houses huddle round the old church of **St-Marcel** and its beautiful bell-tower. The **Butte de Montenoison** makes a good stopping-off point for drivers wishing to stretch their legs. At an altitude of 417m (1,368ft), it is the highest point in the Nivernais region and offers a fine view over the Morvan.

The old timber rafting town of **Clamecy** (pop. 6,000) lies in the Yonne *département* at the confluence of the Beuvron and the Yonne. Many of the half-timbered houses are crooked and bowed and the roofs are covered in moss. The town's *Syndicat d'Initiative* or tourist office is housed in one of these gems in Rue de la Promenade. The narrow, cobbled **Rue de la Monnet** leads downhill past a series of crooked house walls. In Rue Bourgeoisie, the **Musée d'Art et d'Histoire Romain Rolland** is devoted not only to the life and work of the Clamecy-born writer Romain Rolland (*see page 72*), but also to European painting from the 17th century and the history of timber floating for which the town was renowned.

Clamecy's Rue de la Monnet

Follow the Yonne Valley via **Châtel-Censoir** to **Le Saussois**, whose most striking feature is the bizarrely-formed, bright limestone rocks above the river, a popular spot for climbers wishing to practise their skills.

Continue northwards along the Yonne Valley past the little town of **Mailly-le-Château** and on to **Cravant**. From here, **Auxerre** (*see page 53*) lies to the northwest and **Avallon** (*see page 52*) to the southeast.

St-Seine l'Abbaye

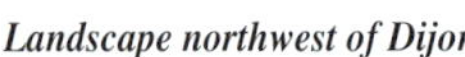

Route 6

Churches, monasteries and brave Celts

On a history trail through northern Burgundy (460km/285 miles) *see map on pages 36–7*

All that is missing is a veiled maiden at a window in the tower and the scene would be set for an epic tale of knights and bravery. But it is not only the picture postcard town of Semur-en-Auxois that can boast a medieval past. Evidence of the region's important place in history can be seen throughout the two *départements* of Côte d'Or and Yonne. In the shady cloisters of ancient monasteries or the cool tranquillity of the grand churches and cathedrals, the impression can easily be gained that very little sand has passed through the hour-glass.

Landscape northwest of Dijon

On the RN71 just such a scene is visible to the northwest of Dijon. In a concealed dip surrounded by an idyllic landscape of woods and pastures, **St-Seine-l'Abbaye** suddenly appears. The impressive tower on the 13th-century church could, from a distance, easily be mistaken for a fortified castle. A huge portal set in a weathered and crumbling facade gives access to the church. It takes a while to adjust to the gloom, before the damp chill of the Middle Ages gradually becomes apparent. Faint shafts of light penetrate the 800-year-old rose window in the chancel. On the transept wall hangs a burial plaque for an abbot, portrayed as a skeleton.

Outside the town, the road climbs to a picnic spot that provides a view over the rolling countryside, only 10km (6 miles) from the source of the Seine.

As far as the area around Fouilles Alésia, narrow, asphalted country lanes lead off through farmland to tiny villages where, if it were not for the rooftop satellite dishes and agricultural machinery in the farmyards, a horse and cart would not look out of place.

★ **Flavigny-sur-Ozerain** sits on the crest of a hill which drops steeply on three sides. In comparison with some other villages, this one can at least boast that it looks pretty and smells nice. It is the monks who lived here over 1,000 years ago that the townsfolk must thank for the pleasant aniseed aroma that pervades the town. The delicious sweets are now made by machines in a small factory which welcomes visitors. Balls of sugar are created in dozens of rotating mixing machines and these are then sprayed with the distinctively-flavoured essence of aniseed.

The remains of the **Abbaye St-Pierre**, which was founded around 719, are worth seeking out. The 9th-century St-Rein crypt, the oldest section, has been restored. Several of the capitals display flower motifs or figures. Apart from the crypt, only a hexagonal chapel remains from the former monastery.

Modern buildings are hard to find in Flavigny, and the peace and tranquillity are disturbed only by the occasional tourist. Few of the houses are equipped with electric door-bells and the residents rely on the weight of decorative cast-iron door-knockers. Access to one of the old town gates, the **Porte du Bourg**, used to be via a drawbridge.

★ **Alise-Ste-Reine** spreads up the sides of the 400-m (1,300-ft) Mont Auxois. On this hill in 52BC a battle was fought that had a considerable bearing on the course of European history. Caesar's soldiers defeated the troops of the Celtic prince Vercingetorix, heralding the start of 400 years of Roman occupation in Gaul. Vercingetorix was captured by the Romans, taken to Rome and then, after six years in prison, murdered. The sculptor Aimé Millet has immortalised Vercingetorix. The 7-m (23-ft) bronze giant with flowing locks now covered by a patina grimly surveys the battlefield. Maybe he is pondering the words that Napoleon claims Caesar spoke to Vercingetorix: 'A united Gaul, forming a single nation, moved by the same spirit, could defy the universe.'

The excavation site at **Fouilles Alésia** was once a prosperous Gallo-Roman town with a theatre dating from the 2nd century AD and a Merovingian basilica, dedicated to St Regina. Regina is said to have been condemned to death in the middle of the 3rd century as she refused to marry the Roman governor Ulibrius. According to legend, at the site where she met her death, water miraculously started to flow from the ground and every year on 7 September pilgrims pay homage to St Regina at the spring.

Flavigny-sur-Ozerain

47

Vercingetorix

Semur-en-Auxois

Eglise Notre-Dame

48

There is hardly another place in Burgundy as picturesque as the small, medieval town of ★★ **Semur-en-Auxois** (pop. 5,400), which lies in a loop of the River Armançon. The **Pont Joly** to the north of the town centre was built in 1786. It is situated beneath a townscape of squat round towers, fortified house fronts and old tiled roofs, crossing a natural moat which flows past small gardens and lush green embankments.

The rich vegetation goes back to the 16th century. At that time every young married couple was obliged to plant two tree shrubs. **Pont Pinard** is another favourite with photographers. The best shot includes the bridge, houses packed on to a steep slope and the Notre-Dame church reflected in the waters of the Armançon.

Given its position as a natural fortress, people sought protection here long before the town was founded in the Middle Ages. A crack in the **Tour de l'Orle d'Or** extending from the eaves to the foundations appeared during a siege of the town in 1589. At the time the roof was covered in pure gold. Now in use as a local and natural history museum, the tower has only survived intact because the walls are a massive 5m (18ft) thick.

Surrounded by fine old houses, **Place Notre-Dame** to the east of the town centre exudes medieval charm. It is overlooked by the ★ **Eglise Notre-Dame** which was started in the 13th century on Romanesque foundations and not completed until well into the 16th century. The tympanum of the 13th-century **Porte des Bleds** on the north front is a particularly outstanding feature. It shows scenes from the life of St Thomas. Inside in the Lazarus chapel, there is an impressive burial scene dating from the 15th century.

Epoisses lies 12km (7 miles) to the west of Semur-en-Auxois. The villagers are naturally proud of the aromatic cheese that is produced here. But the sight that attracts the tourists has nothing to do with the well-known cheese. A huge dovecote in the ★ **château** here has room for 3,000 birds. It was built to accommodate its feathered guests in the 16th century (exterior open all the year round, 9am–7pm; interior 1 July to 30 September, 9am–noon and 3–6pm). The château was once used by Henri IV and Madame de Sévigné.

★★★ **Abbaye de Fontenay** lies in a wooded valley outside the small town of Montbard (daily 9am–noon and 2–6pm; guided tours in English). For the past 800 years, this Cistercian monastery has led an isolated existence, in accordance with the teachings of the father of the order, Bernard de Clairvaux. Since the medieval monastery became a UNESCO World Heritage Site, it has had to cater

The château at Epoisses

for the needs of the thousands of visitors who wander around the abbey. Only in the low season does tranquillity return to the old building.

The monastery was founded by Bernard de Clairvaux in 1118, two decades after Robert de Molesme had established the Cistercian order. For de Molesme the original principals of St Benedict, i.e. 'pray and work', were being flouted in a decadent and extravagant way.

A first glance behind the walls of the monastery reveals the plain west facade of the abbey church which was consecrated by Pope Eugene in 1147. It symbolises the strength and clarity of the monks' simple life here. Pillars for the 66-m (220-ft) long nave rise out of the well-trampled shingle floor up into the gloomy barrel vaulting, illuminated only by light from the chancel windows.

A staircase leads up into the huge, unheated dormitory where, after a hard day's work in the fields or in the smithy, the monks would spend half the night. At 1 o'clock, they would be aroused from their deep slumbers on straw mattresses and called to prayer. Beneath the dormitory is the chapterhouse and, next to it, a warming room with two fireplaces. Here the monks, trembling with cold, were allowed to stay for a while and warm up. Their average life expectancy was around 35 years.

Fontenay's cloisters are a splendid example of Cistercian architecture. The arches surrounding this small, square courtyard rest on huge double pillars. The only decorative elements that the builders dared to include are the stylised leaf capitals.

★ **Vix**, 6km (4 miles) north of **Châtillon-sur-Seine**, only came to prominence when its stunning archaeological finds hit the international headlines. According to recent evidence, far more people lived here in the 6th century BC than now, as it was probably one of the most important

Abbaye de Fontenay

Young visitors

market towns in Gaul. Excavations in and around this Celtic town by Mont Lassois have unearthed over a million fragments of pottery, hundreds of clasps and brooches, weapons and ornaments. But the real treasures are the grave offerings found beside a Celtic princess. Her skeleton lay on a state chariot and she was bearing a magnificent gold tiara. Most of the other artefacts were of Greek or Etruscan origin, including what is now known as the Vix vase. This huge bronze goblet in the shape of an amphora, 1.8m (6ft) high and weighing 208kg (459lbs), could hold about 1,200 litres (265 gallons) of wine. It is decorated with a frieze of Greek war chariots and the handles show Medusa, the female monster from Greek mythology. Usually she is shown with snakes in her hair, but here they replace her arms and legs.

The vase and other treasures can be seen in the **Musée de la Société Archéologique et Historique du Châtillonais** (7 rue du Bourg; 16 June to 15 September daily 9am–noon and 1.30–6pm, 16 September to 15 November and 11 April to 15 June daily 9am–noon and 2–6pm). As well as the famous treasure, a series of black and white photographs are displayed, documenting the excavations which were conducted by René Joffroy.

About 2,000 years separate the Celtic Vix vase from the Renaissance. The simple and austere castle at ★★ **Ancy-le-Franc** is one of Burgundy's few secular buildings that date from this period (1 April to 11 November daily 10am–noon and 2–6pm). Built in 1546 it was one of the first of its kind in France. The architect, Sebastiano Serlio, came from Bologna and, not surprisingly, this feudal mansion built around an elegant inner courtyard has many Italian features. Inside, the 25 rooms that the visitor may see are superbly decorated and contain many items of valuable furniture from the past four centuries, including a number of Gobelins tapestries.

Ancy-le-Franc, and detail

The ★★ **Château Tanlay** is another jewel from the Renaissance period. Compared to Ancy-le-Franc, this moated mansion with its round towers and domed roofs makes a much more attractive sight. The main building work took place in the 16th century, but it was not fully completed until the 17th century. For the past 300 years, the property, whose main entrance is flanked by two obelisks, has stayed in the hands of the same family, but they are happy to open the doors of their home to the public.

Château Tanlay

Tonnerre (pop. 6,200) was very badly damaged by a fire in the 16th century but, fortunately, the 13th-century **Hôpital de Notre-Dame-des-Fontentilles** survived. The founder of the oldest hospital in France was Marguerite de Bourgogne (1249–1308), the widow of Charles d'Anjou. After the death of her husband she retired to Tonnerre and founded the hospital, hoping that through this act of mercy she would earn herself a place in heaven. Inside, the most striking feature of this combination of hospital ward and church is the barrel-shaped roof timbering, a design which was copied for the Hôtel-Dieu in Beaune. The tomb of the founder lies in a small chapel at the end.

The architect of the church of **St-Pierre** chose the finest location in the town – a rocky terrace overlooking the old town. A spring feeds the **Fosse Dionne**, a circular basin which was probably a shrine in Celtic times; in the Middle Ages, however, it was used as a wash-house.

On a hill above Tonnerre stands the 15th-century **l'Abbaye St-Michel**. Formerly a Benedictine monastery, it is now one of Burgundy's most highly-regarded restaurants (tel: 86 55 05 99). Renunciation and modesty are certainly not qualities valued by today's chefs. Only the finest Burgundian ingredients are served here – and the emphasis is on an imaginative menu. If that is not enough, the small, adjoining hotel is an oasis of opulence.

To the west of Tonnerre lies the Chablis wine region with its two dozen or so communes. **Chablis** itself (pop. 2,400), on the banks of the Serein, is the main town in this white wine paradise. The several fine old houses in the narrow lanes demonstrate that in a commercial sense the Chardonnay grape is always a winner.

If a tour of the vineyards does not appeal, then ★ **Pontigny abbey** lies only a few miles to the north. This Cistercian monastery was built by Hugo de Mâcon in 1114 – four years before Fontenay. An avenue of lime trees leads up to the delightful yellowish-grey ★ **Notre-Dame de l'Assomption** abbey church. Measuring 108m (355ft) in length and 20m (65ft) in height, the nave is huge, but the plain and simple decorations such as the water-lily leaves on the capitals create a harmonious picture. When Thomas Becket was forced to leave England in 1164 after his power struggle with Henry II, he sought asylum here, but when he returned, he was murdered by royal accomplices in Canterbury cathedral on 29 December 1170.

Follow the RN77 south as far as **Auxerre** (*see page 53*) and then continue south to Cravant where the Yonne and the Cure meet. ★★ **Vézelay** (pop. 750) lies close to the source of Cure at the end of a winding valley road. The houses in Vézelay are clustered around a narrow rocky ridge. The village's Grande Rue climbs up the hill which is crowned by the magnificent ★★★ **Basilique Ste-Madeleine**. This site was chosen because of the claim that the remains of Mary Magdalene lay here. In 1120 work started on one of France's grandest Romanesque churches

Tonnerre

51

At work in a Chablis vineyard

Basilique Ste-Madelaine, Vézeley: tympanum detail

52

although the chancel and transept hint at the dawning of the Gothic era. Vézelay's monastery flourished in the decades following the laying of the foundation stone, as Bernard de Clairvaux, Louis VII and his wife, Eleanor of Aquitaine, France's Philippe-Auguste, Richard the Lionheart and the Archbishop of Canterbury all stayed here. But thereafter, dark shadows fell over Ste-Madeleine. The monastery was secularised in 1537 and it suffered badly during the Wars of Religion and the French Revolution. Only when the writer Prosper Merimée (1802–70) set in train an initiative for rebuilding the church – eventually completed by Viollet-le-Duc – was it possible to put a stop to the process of creeping decay. Now the old splendour has been restored. The detail on the grand ★★ **tympanum** at the main entrance and the capitals with scenes from both the Old and New Testaments should be studied closely. Inside, what are said to be the remains of Mary Magdalene are kept in a modern shrine in the crypt.

Avallon clock tower and view

Like Vézelay, ★ **Avallon** (pop. 9,000) lies on a rocky spur above the Cousin Valley. The inhabitants laid out tiny gardens on the terraced embankments beneath the town wall, creating a picturesque, medieval atmosphere that also permeates the old town centre. The church of **St-Lazare** is Avallon's finest historic building. Of particular interest are the two richly decorated west portals, outstanding examples of the sculptors' skills at the end of the Romanesque era. Close to the church, the **Tour d'Horloge**, old fortifications and crooked town houses bear witness to Avallon's medieval past.

Return to Dijon (*see page 16*) along the northern edge of the Morvan to Précy-sous-Thil in the Côte d'Or *département*. Join the *autoroute* here or take a more leisurely drive across country.

Route 7

★★ Auxerre – White wine queen on the River Yonne

Auxerre, the capital of Yonne *département* (pop. 40,000), sometimes leads a double life. On windless days, the outlines of the dignified Gothic St-Etienne cathedral and the proud St-Germain abbey are reflected in the waters of the Yonne, making a second bizarre upside-down world. This white wine centre has other charms, one of which is its delightful riverside location. No wonder that connoisseurs of Burgundy rate Auxerre as a close second to Dijon as the region's finest town.

Auxerre has many charms
St-Etienne

History

Auxerre's roots go back further into history than practically anywhere else in the region. Autricum, a settlement founded by the Celtic Senones tribe, occupied this site on the banks of the Yonne long before the arrival of the Romans. In its pre-Christian days it served as an important staging post on the route from the English Channel to Lyon. Tin mined in Cornwall made its way to southern France via Autricum and trees felled in the vicinity were floated down the Yonne to Paris. The river was later used to supply the capital with cereals and wine. Business flourished at that time and the term Burgundy was applied exclusively to wine shipped in barrels from Auxerre. The establishment of an episcopal see during the Middle Ages also helped the town to develop as a regional centre. The tomb of the fifth bishop Germain (c 378–448), who was later canonised, became a place of pilgrimage.

City on the River Yonne

For many centuries, the inhabitants suffered assaults by Germanic tribes, Franks, Huns, Saracens and Normans, before a protective wall was built; the market town received its charter in 1223. In 1358, during the Hundred Years' War, the English attacked the town and it was not until 1477 that it returned to French rule. The region's vineyards were badly damaged by mildew and phylloxera during the second half of the 19th century and it is true to say that the town and its surroundings have still not fully recovered from that catastrophe. In the last century, the vineyards of the Yonne *département* covered an area of 40,000ha (99,000 acres). In 1945 only 1,000ha (2,500 acres) were used for growing grapes. This figure has doubled since then and the high reputation of Chablis wines has helped to put Auxerre back on the wine map of France.

Town tour

For a picture-postcard view of Auxerre, there is no better place than the banks of the River Yonne. **Pont Paul-Bert ❶**, therefore, makes a good starting-point for a tour of the town. This bridge offers a splendid panorama which includes the barges, cruise boats and yachts moored at the riverside against a backdrop of imposing church facades. It is as if the town planners had deliberately sought to create the perfect snapshot.

Aspects of St-Etienne

Quai de la République runs northwards beneath spreading trees along the west bank of the river as far as the **Maison du Tourisme** and only yards away from the ★ **Cathédrale St-Etienne ❷** in **Place St-Etienne**. This spot by the Yonne was regarded as sacred as long ago as the 5th century AD. Three different buildings occupied the site, before bishop Guillaume de Seignelay commissioned the present building in 1215. In the four centuries that followed, architects created a west front that resembles petrified lacework. According to the original plans, the church was to have two towers, but after the completion of the 70-m (220-ft) north tower, the money ran out. Look out for both the single statues and the groups of figures on the facade. These engaging tableaux depict events from the life of John the Baptist (on the right portal) and the fate of the Virgin Mary. Themes such as the Flood and the Creation are represented on the left portal, while on the tympanum above the middle *Portail du Jugement Dernier* (Last Judgement portal) Christ rests on the world, flanked by Mary and John. The three portals show clear signs of vandalism. In 1567 Protestants angrily destroyed part of the decoration on this Catholic church.

The oldest part of the cathedral, a triple-naved crypt from the first half of the 11th century, is of great inter-

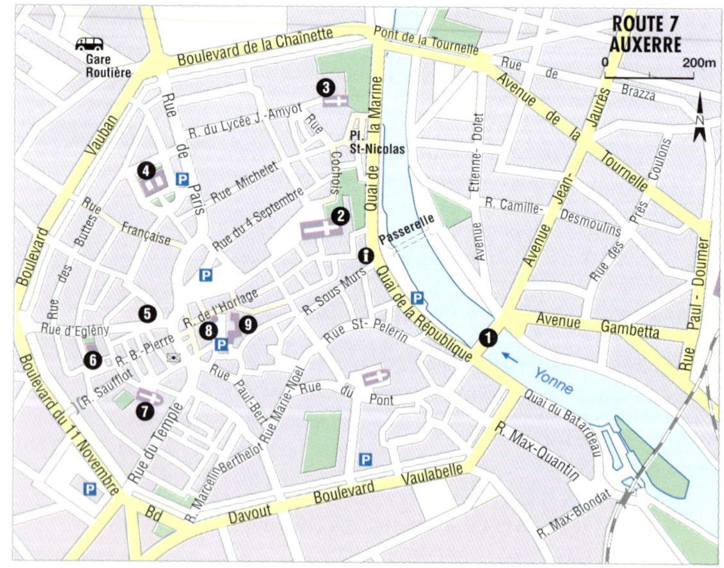

est, primarily because of the Romanesque frescoes in the apse vaulting. This apocalyptic painting shows Christ on a white horse accompanied by four angels, also on horseback. Who painted this mainly ochre-coloured mural is not known. Manuscripts, books of hours and enamelling dating from the 12th and 13th centuries are exhibited here.

By **Quai de la Marine** outside the Abbaye St-Germain, half-timbered houses, crooked with age, ring the **Place St-Nicolas**, which has a fountain at its centre. A statue of St Nicholas surveys the paved square from a niche in a weathered house front. Nearby, a narrow street leads up to the former **St-Germain** abbey church ❸. This church and monastery school were founded in the 6th century by Clotilda, the wife of the Frankish king Clovis, and were built over the grave of St Germain. Of most interest is the crypt, which was begun in 841 and consecrated 24 years later. As one of the most important Carolingian monuments in France, it is now part of the **Musée St-Germain** (access to crypt only as part of a guided tour; Wednesday to Monday 9am–12.30pm and 2–6.30pm). A passage leads through a number of chapels into a chamber with a natural rock floor. Among the tombs of various dignitaries lies St Germain's sarcophagus and shrine.

Rue de Paris passes in front of the **Palais de Justice** ❹, a 19th-century building by the architect, Piéplu, before reaching the town centre and the oldest house in Auxerre. The **Hôtel du Cerf-Volant** ❺ in **Place Robillard** dates from the 14th century. **Musée Leblanc-Duvernoy** ❻ is housed in an elegant classical building nearby (9bis rue d'Eglèny). Exhibits include 18th-century Gobelins tapestries, paintings dating from the 17th century to the present day, pottery, *faiences* and furniture.

St-Eusèbe ❼ (Place St-Eusèbe) with its 12th-century tower is often eclipsed by the more illustrious St-Etienne and St-Germain churches. Nevertheless, many visitors come to Auxerre just to see the 1,000-year-old blue silk cloth decorated with two eagles in which the body of St-Germain was wrapped.

Auxerre was protected by a wall even in Roman times. There were several gates and one of them can still be seen in **Rue de l'Horloge**. It was built in the 15th century on the foundations of the original gate. Late Gothic in style, the **Tour de l'Horloge** ❽, with its pencil-tip tower, adds to the charm of the medieval townscape.

The nearby **Place de l'Hôtel de Ville** is surrounded by half-timbered houses, some dating back 400 years. The classical **Hôtel de Ville** ❾ itself was built in 1733. Not far from the Tour de l'Horloge, a vaulted passage leads to Place Maréchal-Leclerc where a plaque recalls Cadet Roussel (1743–1807), a local man whose blighted ambitions are remembered in a famous French song.

Place St-Nicolas

Café life

55

Stained glass in St-Eusèbe

The market hall in Joigny

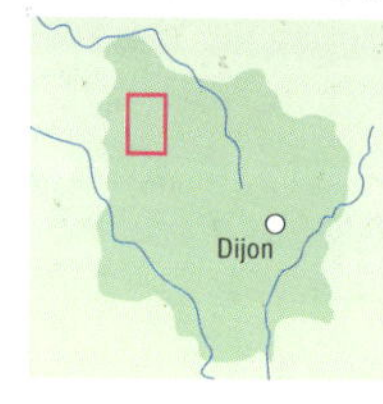

56

Route 8

Between the Yonne and the Loire

Round trip from Auxerre to Sens and through the Puisaye district (200km/124 miles)

'The charm, the pleasure of this part of the country, with its hills and valleys, valleys so narrow that they could almost be gorges, is the woodland ...the deep and all-embracing woodland, where trees sway and tremble as far as the eye can see…' These are just some of the words the writer Colette used to described her native Puisaye, a remote region which lies between the Yonne and the Loire. It is not an area that has played an important part in history, but woodcutters, potters and charcoal burners have made good use of the local resources. Although rather off the beaten track, La Puisaye has recently become popular with city dwellers seeking refuge from the stresses and strains of modern life.

Barely 30km (20 miles) north of Auxerre lies **Joigny** (pop. 12,000), a compact medieval town on the banks of the Yonne. Behind the uninspiring riverside rises a golden town covered in jagged brown tiles. Joigny suffered a great fire in 1530 and was rebuilt in stone. The houses are laid out in terraces on a long, narrow hill overlooking the river, with the two churches of **St-Jean** and **St-Thibault** dominating the skyline.

Market days are Saturday and Wednesday, but Saturday morning is the best time of week to see the town in full swing. In the market hall by the Yonne bridge, vegetable stalls are piled high with shiny apples and crisp lettuces. Elsewhere, discerning shoppers inspect the black-

Try some local honey

footed Bresse chickens, local wines and cheeses, freshly-cut hams and a wide range of sausages.

Rue Gabriel-Cortel climbs up from the Yonne bridge into the old town, passing modern shop windows framed by carved house timbers. Several half-timbered houses escaped the blaze of 1530 and retain their naive carvings of foliage, grapes and garlands. In **Rue de la Galère** and **Rue du Loquet**, the crooked facades look as though they were built without a plumb line or a spirit-level.

Savour the medieval atmosphere around **Place de Pilori** where in the Middle Ages criminals were subjected to public ridicule in the stocks. With carvings of monks and knights and crossbeams in the shape of crocodiles, **Maison Pilori** has by far the finest facade. Few visitors can resist a quick tour of the 11th-century church of **St-Thibault** to see the statue of the **Smiling Madonna** (fourth pillar on the right facing the pulpit).

Maison Pilori, facade detail

On the edge of Joigny by the road to Sens stands the famous **La Côte St-Jacques** restaurant (tel: 86 62 09 70). The glittering chandelier at the entrance indicates that this is no ordinary restaurant. Praise and distinctions have been heaped on the culinary skills of the *chef de cuisine* for years now. From the apéritif through to the dessert, food writers and gourmets continue to give the cooks the highest accolade. A tunnel links the restaurant with the neighbouring luxury hotel.

Proud chef, La Côte St-Jacques

57

With ★★ **Sens** (pop. 27,000) so far away from Dijon and the vineyards of Burgundy, it is easy to forget that the town is in fact part of the old duchy. A glance in a history book will reveal that the Senones, a Celtic tribe that lived by the Yonne in the 4th century BC, had a lasting influence on the course of European history. Hordes of Senones and other Celtic tribes under the leadership of Brennus invaded Italy and seized Rome in 387BC and then headed east to Asia Minor to found an independent kingdom. The name of the town is the only surviving reminder of these adventurous peoples who were eventually suppressed by Caesar between 54 and 52BC. Nothing remains of the huge walls that the Romans built around the town – according to legend they were held together with gold chains.

What is apparent, however, is that Sens was for centuries the seat of a powerful archbishop and the ★★ **Cathédrale St-Etienne** in Place de la République remains as a symbol of that power. This is one of the oldest Gothic cathedrals in France, and also one of the finest. The three west portals stand out

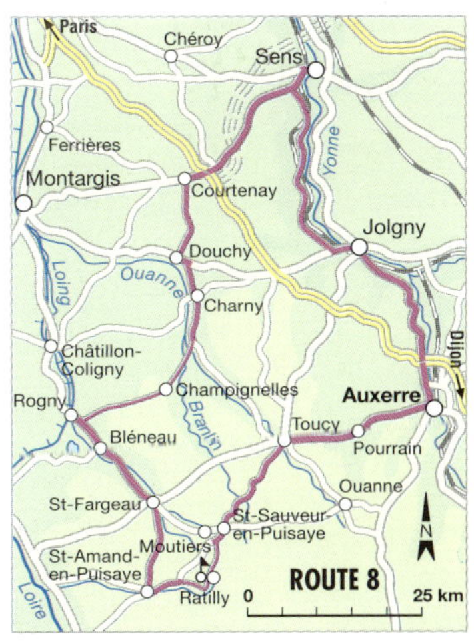

as the highlights of the building while inside, the dimensions of the 113-m (370-ft) long nave make a greater impact. The stained-glass windows in the ambulatory and transept depict biblical stories and legends about the saints. Archbishop Henri Sanglier was responsible for commissioning the cathedral in around 1140 when an ecumenical council was taking place. A year before the imposing structure was consecrated by Alexander III, this Pope who bitterly opposed the power of the Hohenstaufen dynasty, installed himself in exile in Sens and declared his new residence to be the capital of Christianity – a difficult concept to comprehend as a distinctly provincial atmosphere prevails in the old town today.

In the 13th century, the **Palais Synodal** and **Archbishop's Palace** were built along the south facade of the cathedral and these are now home to a museum. On display here are archaeological finds, a variety of Gallo-Roman exhibits and a breathtaking treasure of religious art which is probably unsurpassed in value and splendour anywhere in France.

*Ancient hardware in the
Archbishop's Palace*

58

Three of a kind

Rogny-les-Sept-Ecluses

Sens is the last urban centre on this route. From now on, rural seclusion, woods, fields, hamlets and villages dominate the view from the often deserted road. In contrast to the Côte d'Or vineyards, **La Puisaye**, as this region between the Yonne and the Loire is called, is a relatively poor part of France with a population that only makes a meagre living off the land.

To complement a meandering drive through the Puisaye, try to visit a *ferme auberge*, a real farmhouse serving hearty local fare, now sadly something of an endangered gastronomic species. In the village of **Champignelles** south of Sens, Les Perriaux is one such *ferme auberge* that has survived (July/August daily; mid-September to June Friday evening to Sunday lunch, tel: 86 45 13 22). The proprietors serve up generous portions of home-made food including dishes made with genuine free-range chickens.

Rogny-les-Sept-Ecluses is named after the seven locks which were built on the Briare canal at the beginning of the 17th century by Henri IV. They overcome the 34-m (110-ft) difference between the Trézée Valley and the Le Loing Valley.

The village of **St-Fargeau** (pop. 1,700) with its narrow, winding streets, lies in the shadow of a castle (15th–17th century). One of its most famous residents was Anne-Marie-Louise d'Orléans, the cousin of the Sun King Louis XIV. This *Grande Mademoiselle* made no secret of her sympathy for the Fronde, a movement supported by the nobility and parliament that opposed the absolutism of the

17th century. The court of Versailles took exception to her views and banished her to St-Fargeau from 1652 to 1657 and from 1662 to 1664. With the help of the architect François Le Vau, she transformed the dilapidated building into a comfortable residence.

St-Armand-en-Puisaye would be nothing more than an anonymous provincial village were it not for the *Centre national d'initiation, de formation et de perfectionnement de la poterie et du grès* or, more succinctly, France's national pottery school. One of its principal aims is to ensure the continued existence of this traditional Puisaye craft. Courses are offered to both beginners and more advanced students.

Pottery student, St-Armand-en-Puisaye

At the entrance to the 700-year-old **Château de Ratilly** near Treigny, ivy scrambles up the outside walls of the vast side towers. This isolated fairy-tale castle is surrounded by a moat, now sadly overgrown with grass and weeds. Since 1951 when the property changed hands, concerts and other cultural events have been held here.

Château de Ratilly

Evidence of La Puisaye's traditional crafts can also be found in **Moutiers**. A huge kiln with a capacity of 75 cubic metres (2,650 cubic feet) is on display to the public. For further information contact François Solano, La Bâtisse, tel: 86 45 55 50. The village church has also provided an unusual insight into the region's distant past. In 1982 after a very dry spring, the churchgoers were startled to see the colour of the church walls change. But their surprise turned to amazement when, from under the peeling paint, an ochre-coloured fresco emerged. This has now been uncovered in full and it is thought that the section in the nave dates from the 12th or 13th century and the section by the altar from the 16th century.

The church fresco in Moutiers

The emergence of this medieval fresco raised many local people's awareness of the part the powdery mixture of iron oxides played in the region's history. The earth-brown pigment was found and used in several places in the Puisaye. It was exported to Holland in the 18th century and, when the railways opened up the European market, it was also sold to Russia.

An imposing keep that once formed part of a 12th-century wall built by the counts of Auxerre and Nevers is one reason for including **St-Sauveur-en-Puisaye** in the itinerary, but the writer Colette (*see page 72*) is also responsible for attracting tourists here. She was born and brought up in this village, although the family home in Rue Colette is owned privately.

Return to Auxerre via **Pourain**, a town that was a major source of ochre until well into the 19th century. The paintings in the **Chapelle St-Baudel** demonstrate why this substance was prized so highly by artists.

59

Route 9

A round tour through southern Burgundy

Chalon-sur-Saône – Tournus – Cluny – Mâcon – Paray-le-Monial – Chalon-sur-Saône (280km/174 miles)

Open all hours

Hints of brown, ochre and matt green in the rural landscape foretell the approach of autumn. The farmer's wife tidies up in the garden. Early in the morning, the farmer anxiously inspects his dew-covered grapes in the vineyard. From a distance, some of the little villages resemble castles, with strong Romanesque towers at their hearts pointing heavenwards like God's stone finger. In the Mâconnais, stout pillars support the dignified medieval architecture, creating a cool and sombre atmosphere in the gloomy interiors of the Romanesque churches.

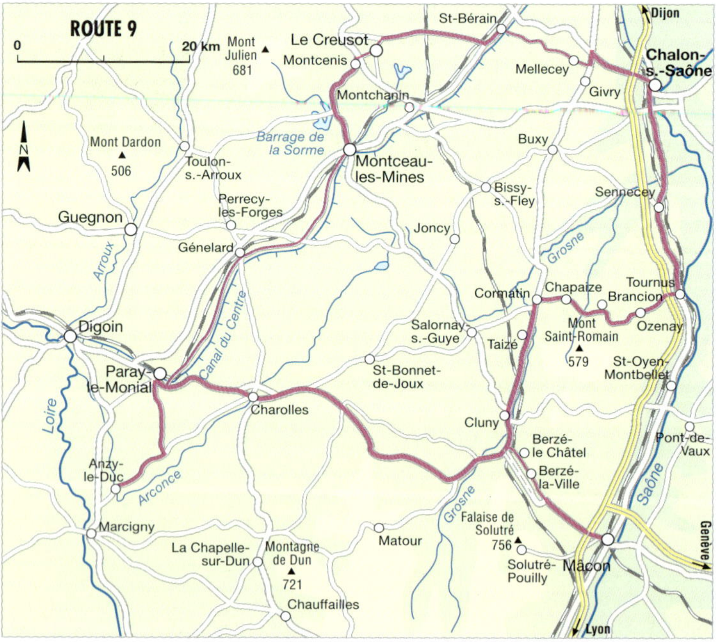

Chalon-sur-Saône (pop. 54,500) is situated close to the busy motorway that links Paris with Mediterranean and this has helped to create a flourishing centre for commerce and industry, with bottle-making one of the town's contributions to the local wine trade. However, Chalon's origins go back to long before the construction of the *autoroute*, probably to the 3rd century BC. Later on, its geographical position by the banks of the Saône became an important factor in encouraging commerce. In the 6th and 7th centuries, it was the seat of the Frankish Burgundian kings, but invasions, sackings and destruction, not to mention a terrible plague, led to a decline that was not reversed until the 16th century.

The lively **Place de l'Hôtel de Ville** is the best place to begin a walk around the town. Casting its shadow over the square is one of the few baroque buildings in Burgundy, the church of **St-Pierre**. In the 18th century, an Ursuline convent was situated diagonally opposite, but it now houses the **Musée Denon**. Dominique Vivant Denon (1747–1825) was born here and enjoyed an eventful life as a diplomat. He served initially in Switzerland, Italy and St Petersburg. After the French Revolution he set himself up as a fashion designer, at the end of the 18th century he accompanied Napoleon to Egypt as a war engraver and, finally he was responsible for the removal of plundered art treasures to Paris. As well as prehistoric and Gallo-Roman archaeological finds, sacred art and 17th- to 19th-century paintings are also exhibited here.

Inside Chalon's Musée Denon

To the east of the town hall square lies the **Rue au Change** pedestrian precinct. The modern shop windows set in old facades seem out of place in the historic town centre. **Maison Colason** (No 3) with its two medallions and iron balcony balustrades is just one such example. In **Rue du Chatelet**, another shopping street, **Maison des Quatre Saisons** (No 37) with its renderings of the four seasons and stone water spout dates from 1657. The four corner houses at the junction of **Rue du Chatelet** and **Grande Rue** combine to create a delightful picture.

The precinct leads to the old and, in places, tastefully restored houses surrounding **Place St-Vincence**. When renovation work was carried out, half-timbering was discovered underneath the rendering and thus now adds to the medieval atmosphere around the square. Many of the ground-floor premises are shops but their modern, brightly painted wooden facades are nevertheless in keeping with the rest of the square. Considering that the **Cathédrale St-Vincence** took five centuries to build, it displays a largely unified style. Long before the cathedral was built, a temple dedicated to the Roman god Mercury stood on this site.

Cathédrale St-Vincence

Returning via the **Quai de la Poterne**, the **Pont St-Laurent** crosses the Saône, offering a fine view of the riverbanks. Only a few yards away at 28 quai des Messageries is the **Musée Niepce** which is devoted to the life and work of the early photographer Nicéphore Niepce (*see page 72*).

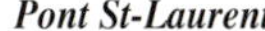
Pont St-Laurent

With its narrow, winding streets and alleys, low house entrances and ageing facades, ★★ **Tournus** (pop. 6,600) would be no different from all the other smallish towns

St-Philibert

of Burgundy, were it not for the church of ★★ **St-Philibert** in the heart of the old town, a monument which – together with Dijon's St-Bénigne – provided a model for many Romanesque churches. When viewed from the main thoroughfare, the tall west front made from stone blocks of varying sizes can be glimpsed between two massive fortified towers. It is hard to ignore the peculiar charm of this simple and yet impressive church.

During the 6th century Tournus, situated on the Roman Via Agrippina between Lyon and Trier, was a place of pilgrimage. The faithful came here to honour St Valerian who died a martyr's death in the 2nd century. An abbey was later established. In 836 it became a refuge for the monks of St-Philibert-de-Noirmoutiers on the Atlantic coast, who had fled before the Norman invaders, taking with them the bones of their saint. At the beginning of the 10th century their successors started work on a church but it was destroyed by invading Hungarians in 937. In the middle of the 10th century the monks started work again, but this time the church fell victim to a fire and only the crypt survived. Work restarted in 1007 with the present church using the crypt's foundations. The crossing tower was completed in the 12th century.

The west front has a distinctly fortified look as its huge walls consist of coarse-hewn stone blocks, small windows and openings like arrow loops. Walls in the narthex are decorated with 14th-century frescoes. A staircase leads up to the Chapelle St-Michel and from here it is possible to view the symmetrical triple-naved interior with its different vaulting styles, supported by huge pillars of yellowish stone. The three chapels in the ambulatory probably originate from the church's 10th-century predecessor. Some 12th-century wall paintings are visible in the crypt and these are as well preserved as the capitals which, in a stylistic sense, resemble those in the crypt at St-Bénigne in Dijon. On the south side a wine cellar and a refectory overlook the cloisters.

The **Musée Perrin-de-Puycousin** in Place de l'Abbaye recreates the everyday life of earlier centuries. Displays include lace from Cluny, kitchen utensils, 18th-century furniture and costumes from various parts of the region.

Musée Perrin-de-Puycousin

Ozenay castle

West of Tournus the D14 winds its way up the **Col de Beaufer**. Beyond the pass in the village of **Ozenay** stands a castle whose owners must have had a soft spot for the architectural style of distant Lombardy. Tiny villages with huge, old farmsteads concealed behind entrances overgrown with ivy are typical features of the timeless Mâconnais countryside.

Brancion (pop. 150) is perched on top of a rocky spur high above the geometric field patterns. In the 11th cen-

62

tury the village's lords joined in the rebellion against the abbots of Cluny and the counts of Chalon and the partly destroyed fortifications are a testimony to their influential role. On a clear day from the restored keep it is possible to see the Morvan mountains and the Autun region. Of more interest than the ramparts of this once mighty fortress is the delightful Romanesque church of **St-Pierre**. Unusual features in the left side aisle and chancel apses are the Gothic frescoes which were painted during the 14th century in the reign of Odo IV. Those in the chancel show an enthroned Christ as well as scenes from the Resurrection. In the left-hand aisle it is possible to make out Abraham taking two souls to his bosom. The rocky spur ends abruptly outside the church. The view from here encompasses **La Chapelle-sous-Brancion** at the foot of the hill and the distant countryside.

All buildings in Briancon are finished with rough-hewn stone blocks. Along the bumpy roads the walls are overgrown with ivy and the stonework encased in moss and lichen. In this medieval setting, the moderately-priced **Auberge du Vieux Brancion** restaurant could easily be mistaken for an old market hall. In the summer, there are three different menus to choose from.

The Romanesque **St-Martin** church at **Chapaize** draws many visitors. Unlike other early Romanesque buildings in Burgundy, it displays clear Italian influences. Its groundplan, decorations and also the bell-tower bear distinct similarities with the Lombardian *campaniles*. The abbots of St-Pierre in Chalon probably commissioned the church and they had good contacts with Abbot Guglielmo da Volpiano, an architect of Italian origin who was responsible for many fine abbeys in both France and Italy. The oldest sections of the church, such as the impressive round

St-Pierre's Gothic frescoes

Brancion ramparts

63

The view from Brancion

pillars in the interior, are thought to date from before 1030. Many alterations took place in later centuries, but the early Romanesque outline remains unchanged.

As in many other French country mansions, the magnificent interiors of **Château Cormatin** have been skilfully concealed from the public gaze by sober-looking walls. Anyone who crosses its threshold will be overwhelmed by the baroque extravagance of the Louis XIII-style suites of rooms and staircases.

Château Cormatin

The peace and tranquillity of the Grosne Valley around Cormatin is disturbed in the spring when young people from all over Europe descend on **Taizé**. The Easter gathering here attracts young Christians from a wide range of denominations. At other times of the year, this religious community, where about 80 Catholic and Protestant brothers from 20 or so different countries live and work, encourages unity and reconciliation among young people. A printing press, pottery, other workshops and the surrounding land play their part in sustaining the community and its international mission.

The Taizé community was founded by Roger Schutz, a Swiss pastor who came to this abandoned farm in 1940 and established his own order. As a committed Protestant, he believed deeply in the unity of all Christian churches and set about trying to bring reconciliation between the various groupings. Taizé began as a hiding place for members of the Resistance and those escaping Nazi persecution, but since then more than 2 million young people have made their way here to take part in discussions and prayers. The visitors stay in tents or very basic accommodation and, for their board, pay a sum in line with their income.

Taizé: a community for the young

The famous abbey at ★★ **Cluny** (pop. 4,700), a beacon of Christianity and a citadel of spirituality and culture, was founded in the final years of the first millennium BC. After the moral decay of the whole clergy, including the Vatican, had set in, it was here at Cluny that the important reform movement within the Catholic church and the monasteries began. The concept of a crusade, the *reconquista* in Spain and the renewal of the monasteries in accordance with the teachings of St Benedict of Nursia (480–542) all originated in Cluny, the largest monastery ever built in the western world. Cluny's designers developed the idea of a building on an east-west axis in the shape of a Latin cross with a bayed chancel at the eastern end. In 1626 the abbey church of **St-Pierre-et-St-Paul** lost its title as the greatest sacred building in Christendom – acquired on its completion in 1130 – with the reconstruction of St Peter's in Rome. Sadly, only a section of the southern transept remains.

Cluny: beacon of Christianity

64

Before the secularisation that followed the French Rev-olution, Cluny administered a monastic empire stretching across the whole of western Europe. In the middle of the 12th century, some 460 monks worked in Cluny alone; a further 10,000 obeyed its authority in about 1,400 af-filiated monasteries. Cluny's influence and wealth started to wane in the 14th century, a time that was characterised by the decadence of the abbots and monks. In the 16th cen-tury many of the former monastery buildings were dis-mantled and the stones used by builders. The site was later sold to a speculator from Mâcon for 2 million francs and by 1823 little remained, apart from what is now visible. From the remnants that are left, including the impressive belltower, it is still possible to obtain some idea of the imposing dimensions which the monastery once boasted. Pieces of the doorway and capitals found during exca-vations, fragments of sculptures, remains of the old library and reconstructions can be seen in the **Musée Ochier** (varying opening times, for details contact Cluny Tourisme, 6 place du Commerce, tel: 85 59 04 84).

Instead of following the main road from Cluny to Mâ-con, take the parallel but much quieter **Circuit Lamar-tine**. **Mâcon** (pop. 37,000) is Burgundy's southernmost town and the brightly-washed facades along **Quai Lamar-tine** on the banks of the Saône have a distinct Mediter-ranean feel, while the view over the red-tiled roofs with the church towers in the background is rather reminis-cent of Florence.

The **Office du Tourisme** in Rue Carnot is the best place to start a tour of the town. It is housed in a tall glass pavil-ion adorned with palms, cacti and other exotic plants. Diagonally opposite, the two towers of the 19th-century church of **St-Pierre** soar upwards. This neo-Romanesque building is of more interest internally than externally. Fres-

Cluny past and present

Mâcon's Quai Lamartine

Maison de Bois, detail

Pont de St-Laurent

coes, the five-part pulpit, the rose window and the organ are all the work of skilled craftsmen. The pedestrianised Rue Carnot leads from the tourist office to **Place aux Herbes** and the **Maison de Bois** (1490–1510), the town's oldest and most famous building. From the first floor, the facade is entirely of wood and many of the window ledges and window frames are decorated with either animal and human figures or geometrical and floral patterns.

During the French Revolution, the poet Lamartine (*see below*) was held in the former Ursuline monastery, but the building now houses the **Musée municipale des Ursulines** (Rue des Ursulines) which displays prehistoric finds from Solutré (*see below*). In **Rue Strasbourg**, the imposing ruins of a double tower are all that remain of the Gothic **Vieux St-Vincence** cathedral, which was destroyed during the French Revolution.

The **Pont de St-Laurent** has spanned the Saône since the 11th century. In the 12th century, a chapel dedicated to St Nicholas stood alongside fortifications in the middle of the bridge, but in subsequent centuries the structure was altered and rebuilt many times in order to allow the passage of larger vessels. Along the promenade on a plinth in front of the **Hôtel de Ville** stands a statue of Mâcon's most famous son. Alphonse Lamartine (1790–1869) ranks alongside Victor Hugo and Stendhal as one of the principal exponents of French Romanticism. He was born in Rue des Ursulines and later lived in what is now Rue Lamartine, where he wrote *Méditations poétiques*. For those who wish to discover more about the famous poet and politician, the **Hôtel Senecé** in Rue Sigorgne contains documents recalling his life's work, as well as some fine tapestries and furniture (daily except Tuesday and Sunday morning, April to October 10am–noon and 2–6pm; November, December and March 2–6pm).

Falaise de Solutré

Near Solutré-Pouilly to the west of Mâcon stands the dramatic 756-m (2,480-ft) **Falaise de Solutré**, which towers above the surrounding countryside like the bow of a sinking ship. This unmistakable symbol of the Mâconnais was the site of some remarkable archaeological finds. The scientist Adrien Arcelin started exploring the region in the 1860s and he reached the conclusion that hunter-gatherers roamed the nearby countryside over 100,000 years ago. Among the most interesting finds were burial grounds, Stone Age weapons, tools and the bones of extinct animals. Countless wild horse bones were found in a deep layer at the base of the rock. At the end of the 19th century it was thought that the horses had been forced to jump off the rock, but this theory is now discounted. It is more likely that they were hunted, trapped at the foot of the rock, killed and then dismembered.

★★ **Paray-le-Monial** (pop. 9,800) lives largely off tourism and pilgrims. After Lourdes, this small town is the most important place of pilgrimage in France. Between 1673 and 1689 Christ is said to have appeared several times before a nun and this is the reason for its popularity among devout Christians. The nun Marguerite-Marie Alacoque (1647–90) was canonised by Pope Benedict XV in 1920 and a festival is held every year on the anniversary of her death, 17 October. Her mortal remains lie in a gilded shrine in the **Chapelle de la Visitation** (Rue de la Visitation). Christ is said to have appeared before her here between 1673 and 1689. Another important date is the second Friday after Whitsuntide when pilgrims attend a ceremony in honour of the Sacred Heart.

The origins of the **Basilique du Sacré-Coeur** (Avenue Jean-Paul III), only a few yards away, date from 1090. There are striking similarities between it and Cluny and these can be explained by the fact that the abbot who commissioned it, Hugo de Semur, used the same team of craftsmen. The interior makes an impressive sight, particularly in the evenings, when the handful of lights create delicate effects and magical shadows. The central nave attains a height of 22m (70ft).

Romanesque architecture is not the only attraction in the town. The Renaissance town hall in Rue de la Paix is one of the prettiest in Burgundy.

About 20 minutes to the southwest in the delightful Brionnais lies the village of **Anzy-le-Duc** with one architectural jewel – a former priory church in Cluniac style. Look carefully at the unusual Romanesque belfry with its three storeys of bays set in an octagonal tower. Inside, the capitals – probably the oldest in Burgundy – are also of interest. Those in the nave show biblical scenes.

Follow the **Canal du Centre** northward towards Burgundy's industrial heartland, the **Bassin Industriel du Creusot**. Iron ore and coal deposits were discovered here in the 16th century and initially these were only exploited in a small way but, by the beginning of the 19th century, they were playing an important part in the burgeoning steel industry. Some of the old factories and machinery have been preserved with a view to attracting tourism.

Le Creusot (pop. 29,000) is at the heart of Burgundy's industrial region. Some 200 years ago cannons were made here, now the famous TGV trains come off the assembly line. In the **Château de la Verrie** in Place Schneider, the **Ecomusée de l'homme et de l'industrie** documents the advance of technology.

The RN70 returns to Chalon-sur-Saône. A longer but more picturesque route passes through the villages of St-Bérain and Mellecey.

Basilique du Sacré-Coeur in Paray-le-Monial

67

Le Creusot: home of TGV trains

Art History

On the trail of prehistory

In the Grottes d'Arcy cave complex near Vézelay, archaeologists have found carved bones and stones proving conclusively that humans lived here at least 100,000 years ago. Other finds include animal drawings on the walls and pieces of broken pottery.

Another discovery was made near Châtillon-sur-Seine in 1953. Archaeologist René Joffroy uncovered an almost completely preserved burial chamber dating from the 6th century BC. The remains discovered inside are thought to be those of a Celtic princess and a delightful bronze vase was one of the artefacts found beside the princess. Known as the 'Vix vase', it was probably made by Greeks in southern Italy.

The Gallo-Roman period

Roman influence in the region spread after Caesar defeated Vercingetorix near Alesia and the culture of the occupying army was soon absorbed by the indigenous Celtic Gauls. Towns were established and, later, Christianity gained a foothold. Augustodunum, modern Autun, became the spiritual, economic, religious and, not least, artistic centre. The remains of the two city gates, Porte St-André and Porte d'Arroux, and also an amphitheatre for 15,000 spectators serve as reminders of the importance of the city during the 400 years of Roman rule.

Architecture

At the beginning of the 4th century, while the Romans still held sway in France, an early Christian artistic style emerged. In the course of the centuries, this style distanced itself from the Roman model, created its own forms and led to what we now call Romanesque architecture. The driving force behind these developments was, of course, the church, principally the Benedictine order, who benefited from William of Aquitaine's decision in 910 to give approval for the construction of a monastery at Cluny. Reforms were initiated here and these led to stricter rules for the monastic orders. As a consequence of the Cluniac reforms, around the middle of the 10th century, the early Romanesque basilica style gained ground. Cluny abbey (II) was followed a few decades later by St-Philibert in Tournus and St-Bénigne in Dijon.

If, in their simplicity, these buildings were an expression of the stricter monastic rules, then the splendid monumental Cluny III, built by Hugo de Semur, demonstrated the increasingly secular nature of the monastery's power.

In 1112 the great Bernard de Clairvaux joined the Cistercian monastery at Cîteaux – founded in 1098 by Robert

Opposite: fine Romanesque sculpture on Autun's Cathédrale St-Lazare

69

Cluny details

St-Bénigne, Dijon

Notre-Dame, Dijon

Ancy-le-Franc

de Molesme – and eventually became the abbot. He was responsible for returning the Romanesque style to ascetic simplicity and the Abbaye de Fontenay is a fine example of his austere vision. The monastery, which was consecrated in 1147, displays no ornamentation, an unnecessary distraction regarded by Bernard as the work of the devil.

During the Romanesque period, many churches were built in southern Burgundy, mainly to the west of a line drawn from Tournus to Mâcon, but the Gothic style which was spreading south from the Ile-de-France only initially gained acceptance in the north of the region.

During the later decades of the 14th century, the extravagant Flamboyant style of the late Gothic era took hold in Burgundy and art in the region came to be dominated by the Flemish masters that Philip the Bold had brought to Burgundy after his marriage to Margaret of Flanders. Examples of their work can be found in the kitchen of the Palais des Ducs in Dijon and the Hôtel-Dieu in Beaune.

The marvellous Loire châteaux were much admired by Burgundian noblemen and these Renaissance-style models were copied during the 16th century. During the rule of François I (1515–47), the skills of Italian craftsmen and architects were often employed. Initially, their designs combined Renaissance features with the still-popular Gothic style, but the châteaux at Ancy-le-Franc, in Sully and in Tanlay are pure Renaissance. St-Michel in Dijon is one of the few church buildings which dates from this period.

Classical forms predominated during the 18th century, particularly in Dijon where many town houses and residences for senior political figures were built. The Hôtel de Vogüé is probably the best example.

Sculpture

The earliest examples of Burgundian sculpture can be seen on the pre-Romanesque leaf capitals in the crypt at Flavigny-sur-Ozerain and in Auxerre's St-Germain. The animal forms and monster heads which decorate the capitals in the crypt of the rotunda in Dijon's St-Bénigne date from a little later.

During the Romanesque period, Cluny abbey became an important centre for European sculpture; however, during the French Revolution many of these works of art were destroyed. There are, nevertheless, a number of places where works by Burgundian religious sculptors can still be found, such as the Ste-Madeleine basilica in Vézelay and Autun's St-Lazare.

When Philip the Bold married Margaret of Flanders, Burgundy did not just expand territorially northward, but the links that were established with Flemish artists led

Tomb of John the Fearless
and his wife at Dijon

to the blossoming of the visual arts. The duke first commissioned the sculptor Jean de Marville to build a tomb but, three years later, a colleague of de Marville, Claus Sluter came to Burgundy from Brussels and in 1389 took charge of the duke's sculpture workshop. His finest achievements are regarded as Philip's tomb, displayed in Dijon's Salle des Gardes, and the statues in the doorway of the Chartreuse de Champmol, also in Dijon.

Sluter died in 1405 and his unfinished works were completed by his cousin Claus de Werve. The funeral procession of pleurants depicted on the base of Philip's sarcophagus and the Well of Moses in the Chartreuse de Champmol are Werve's finest achievements.

François Rude (1784–1855), a famous 19th-century sculptor, came from Dijon and in 1989 his home town established a museum dedicated to his work in the former St-Etienne cathedral. He was a product of the Classical school of sculpture, but became a leading representative of a neo-baroque, naturalist style.

Painting

Burgundian painting never achieved the same grandeur and reputation as the region's architecture or sculpture. Apart from prehistoric cave paintings, the earliest examples of Burgundian brushwork can be found in the form of frescoes in the crypts of St-Germain and St-Etienne in Auxerre. What paintings adorned the walls of the abbey at Cluny before the French Revolution can only be guessed at; however, the Byzantine-influenced frescoes in the former priory church at Anzy-le-Duc have survived and probably date from the 12th century. They were restored in the 19th century.

Literature

Throughout the Middle Ages Burgundian monasteries and churches served not just as places of Christian devotion but also as important cultural centres. In the 12th century, Bernard de Clairvaux wrote a series of theological works and tracts about the way monastic life should be conducted. At the same time, poetry was being written which focused on the life of the medieval knight. Later on, Comines and Olivier de la Manche recorded the deeds of the dukes of Burgundy on paper.

In the 17th century, Jacques-Bénigne Bossuet (1627–1704) from Dijon came to prominence for his acid-tongued obituaries of high-ranking personalities and some of his rhetorical masterpieces were published during his lifetime. More recent literary Burgundian talents include Alphonse de Lamartine (1790–1869), Romain Rolland (1866–1944) and Sidonie-Gabrielle Colette (1873–1954), all of whom have received international acclaim (*see page 72*).

From the Musée François Rude

71

Frescoes in Brancion

Alphonse de Lamartine

Burgundian Heroes

Nicéphore Niepce

Lamartine's works

Sidonie-Gabrielle Colette

The son of a nobleman, **Bernard de Clairvaux** was born in 1090 at the château of Fontaine near Dijon. Bernard had considerable influence on monastic life during the 12th century, primarily because he objected to the luxurious lifestyles and poor discipline of the monks at Cluny. By his example and influence he was instrumental in rescuing the newly-founded monastery at Cîteaux in 1112. He left his mark not just on the spiritual life in the monasteries, but also in the political arena where he treated with emperors, kings and popes. In later life, he was sent to Clairvaux in the Champagne region and charged with the task of developing the Cistercian monastery there. He died in 1153 and was canonised two decades later.

No Burgundian hero has suffered greater neglect than **Nicéphore Niepce** (1765–1833). The world has never recognised his achievements. Only a museum in his birthplace of Chalon-sur-Saône highlights his place in the history of photography. It took him many years to develop his ideas but in 1822 he succeeded in preserving the images of objects on light-sensitive bitumen layers. This pioneering discovery was named Niepcotypie, but nobody acknowledged its significance. Even worse, the episode brought financial ruin to his family.

The name of **Alphonse de Lamartine** (1790–1869) is revered in literary circles around the world. The pain of love led the young poet to put his disappointments and yearnings on paper. As his literary talents developed, he became an important figure in the evolution of French Romanticism. In 1821 he moved into the realm of politics and worked as a diplomat in Italy, before being elected to the French National Assembly in 1831, rising to become Foreign Minister. In later years he returned to writing and died in poverty.

Romain Rolland (1866–1944) was born in Clamecy only three years before the death of Lamartine. Some of his novels are based on the biographies of great artists, such as Handel, Beethoven, Tolstoy and Michelangelo. He was a pacifist and a passionate opponent of nationalism who tried in vain to persuade governments to put their differences to one side. In 1938 Rolland moved to Vézelay where he wrote his revolutionary drama *Robespierre*.

Sidonie-Gabrielle Colette (1873–1954) was born in a small village in the remote Puisaye region of northwest Burgundy. It was place where life had followed an unchanging pattern for centuries – a far cry indeed from her later, eventful life. Colette wrote novels principally for women and she is remembered mainly for the *Claudine* series. Love affairs and the resulting conflicts are abiding themes in her works.

Festivals

Acoustics and acrobatics

January	Festival of St Vincent, with processions in honour of the patron saint of wine producers, takes place on the first Saturday after 22 January in many Côte d'Or villages.
February	High-spirited carnival with parades and balls in Chalon-sur-Saône, Auxonne and Châtillon-sur-Seine.
March	Wine auction in Nuits-St-Georges (sometimes held in April).
May	Horse race and fair in Semur-en-Auxois; wine fair in Mâcon.
June	Classical music festival in Dijon; Sacré-Coeur pilgrimage in Paray-le-Monial, pilgrimage and boatmen's festival in St-Jean-de-Losne; international music festival in Beaune.
July	Jousting on the Yonne in Clamecy; festival of street artists in Chalon-sur-Saône; son-et-lumière show in St-Fargeau château (also August); choir festival in Autun; feast of Ste Magdalene and pilgrimage in Vézelay.
August	Sausage and wine festival in Clamecy; festival in Autun's Roman amphitheatre; music and drama in Semur-en-Auxois; Charolais festival in Saulieu.
September	International folklorique festival in Dijon; pilgrimage in Alise-Ste-Reine.
October	Hot-air ballooning in Auxerre; festival of Ste Marguerite-Marie in Paray-le-Monial.
November	International gastronomy festival in Dijon; 'Les Trois Glorieuses' in Côte d'Or; wine festival in Chablis; jazz festival in Nevers.
December	Christmas markets in several towns.

Food and Drink

Opposite: the evening meal

Burgundian cuisine is highly regarded throughout France; *kir royale*, snails in puff pastry, *boeuf bourguignon* and Bresse chicken are not clever creations from a *nouvelle cuisine* recipe book. All of them are tasty dishes noted for their delicious aroma. In keeping with the peasant traditions of this fertile region, dishes described as *à la bourguignonne* are generally noted more for their use of local produce than for their sophistication. Burgundian chefs are happy to have their cooking described as 'provincial', but the use of this term should not detract from the quality of the food and wine.

Chicken to take home

The land of the aperitif

'A delicious, smooth warm and sweet liqueur which, after the addition of a dash of volcanic Burgundy, strikes the palate with a note of sweetness like the minor trill that ends a Bach fugue'. If gourmets – in this case the Duchess of Clermont-Tonnerre in her 17th-century 'Almanach of Good Food' – go out of their way to make such comparisons in order to describe an aperitif, then what they are describing must be something special and it could be a *kir*. In fact, the discovery of this appetiser at the end of the 19th century probably has something to do with the fact that, at that time, the routinely-drunk table wine was slightly acidic and was improved by the addition of some blackcurrant liqueur. Talk of this sweetening process hardly enhanced the reputation of an important local product and so the mayor of Dijon from 1945 to 1968, a certain Felix Kir, is usually credited with its discovery. He insisted on offering it to guests at all civic receptions. A genuine *kir* should consist of ⅛ to ⅓ of the blackcurrant liqueur known as *cassis* and a dry white Aligoté wine. A *kir royale* is made from *cassis* and champagne or a *Crémant de Bourgogne*, a sparkling white wine that is often drunk on its own as an aperitif.

A story can also be told about the blackcurrant liqueur which is used in *kir*. At the beginning of the 18th century doctors and faith-healers were convinced that it was effective against all types of poisonous bites and stings but, to make up the tincture, the leaves, not the berries were left for a long time in white wine to which had been added a quantity of sugar. *Cassis* is now produced in large quantities and no self-respecting bar in France would be without it.

Burgundian delights

Like every other region of France, fast food outlets exist in Burgundy, but the restaurateurs have stoutly resisted the advance of international junk food.

75

Time for an aperitif

Seafood assortment

Outdoor café

Chefs continue to make a point of using local ingredients: crayfish from the rivers and streams of the Morvan, trout and carp from the lakes, ceps and chestnuts that grow wild in the region's woods, not to mention lean and tender steaks, the beef from the Charolais cattle. The colourful country markets also provide Burgundian cooks with a vast range of seasonal fare.

A meal will generally consist of four courses: hors d'oeuvre, main course, cheese and dessert. On special occasions an additional course, probably a fish dish before the main course, may be included.

Ham in parsley with a sauce made from cream and wine (*jambon persillé*) is a favourite hors d'oeuvre, but a salad with snails and *croûtons* or *andouillettes*, a sausage made from calf's offal is also very popular. *Pôchouse* is a tasty Burgundian fish stew usually consisting of pike, eel, carp, tench and catfish, all simmered in a dry Aligoté. Bread fried in garlic usually floats on the surface.

Carp is often served in a wine sauce (*meurette*) and is best eaten with a chilled white wine. Another Burgundian speciality worth noting is baked carp (*carpe gratinée*). Fish dishes also demonstrate that the local wines are not just delicious to drink but can also be used successfully in cooking, a principle also applied to meat. *Boeuf bourguignon* is a classic meat in wine dish – ideally Charolais beef in red Burgundy, plus carrots, onions, lean bacon, mushrooms and butter all gently casseroled for at least three hours. Before serving, flambé half a glass of *marc de Bourgogne* and wash it all down with a full-bodied red.

The much sought after Bresse chickens come from a part of France which, until the French Revolution, belonged to Burgundy, but which was then divided between the neighbouring *départements*. Since 1919 the sale of the chickens has been subject to strict labelling regulations, rather like the *appellation contrôlée* system for wine. *Poulet à la crème* makes a splendid meal. The various sections of the bird are removed and then cooked slowly in dry white wine and onions. To make the sauce, the liquid is poured off before serving and then mixed with egg yolk and *crème fraîche*. Not a dish for calorie counters.

For the third, or perhaps the fourth course of the meal there are over 20 different regional cheeses to choose from. Both goats' and cows' milk cheeses are on offer and some require both types of milk. In recent years, the Auxois to the north of the Morvan has established itself as an important cheese-producing region. Dairy herds now graze where corn once waved in the wind. Among the most famous Burgundian cheeses are *Ami du Chambertin*, *Epoisses* and *Cîteaux*, as well as the distinctive flavour and aroma of the *Mâcon* and *bouton de culotte* ('trouser button') goats' milk cheeses.

The main course

Burgundy can offer a good variety of desserts. Mouth-watering raspberry sorbet is a marvellous way of rounding off a meal, but more filling is *Belle Dijonnaise*, raspberries soaked in vanilla syrup, blackcurrant ice-cream and toasted almonds.

77

Burgundy's great wines

The wine-making process has probably been known to man for about 5,000 years. The monks from Cluny and the Cistercian monasteries were well-versed in the skills of grape growing. Not only did they plant the vines and crush the fruit, but they shared their knowledge about the cultivation of vines and wine production with the peasants who lived near the monasteries. Over the centuries the area of land used for growing vines gradually increased until the 19th century when disaster struck the Burgundian vineyards. A parasite by the name of *phylloxera vitifoliae* was brought to Europe from North America and it quickly destroyed all the vines in Burgundy. There is still no known insecticide which will kill these tiny creatures but, fortunately, the vine-growers made an invaluable discovery. The rootstocks native to the eastern United States were immune to phylloxera and, eventually, it was possible to graft these phylloxera-resistant rootstocks on to the European wine grape.

The famous vines

Maturing with age

The Burgundian wine-growing region consists of five separate areas. **Chablis** lies to the north in the Yonne *département*. Given the cooler climate and the chalky soil, Chablis wine is closer to champagne than the other wines of Burgundy.

The most famous Burgundies come from the **Côte d'Or**, a 50-km (30-mile) strip on the slopes west of the Saône Valley. The northern vineyards are known as the Côte de Nuits, those in the southern section are called Côte de Beaune. The wines from these vineyards are full-bod-

ied and deep red in colour. Pour a glass of Nuits St Georges to find out exactly what colour 'Burgundy red' is.

The bouquet of many of these wines can take several years to mature, so bottles that bear the name Chambertin-Clos de Bèze, Mazoyères-Chambertin or Mazis-Chambertin are seen by many as investments. The names alone send wine connoisseurs into raptures but the prices of these *grands crus* will frighten off anyone unfamiliar with the wine trade.

At the southern end of the Côte d'Or lies the **Chalonnais**, named after the main town in the area, Chalon-sur-Saône. The famous Aligoté is produced here. It is a dry white wine which, in the opinion of the locals, is best drunk with a little blackcurrant added, i.e. as a *kir*.

The first vines in the **Mâconnais** vineyards were planted by the Benedictine monks of Cluny nearly 1,000 years ago and they continued to tend them until the French Revolution. While Mâcon Supérieur is a very popular red wine from the region, white wines predominate in the south of the Mâconnais.

The southernmost Burgundy wines are produced in the relatively small **Beaujolais** area, most of which is not, strictly speaking, in the Burgundy region. Connoisseurs rate the Beaujolais wines from within Burgundy as the best because of the granite beneath the soil. The Gamay vines from here develop a full and distinctive flavour. Every year in late autumn the Beaujolais Nouveau race makes headlines. This wine is meant to be drunk very young, so the newly-fermented wine is released to the distributors on the third Thursday in November and then spirited to all four corners of the world as quickly as possible. About 40 percent of all Beaujolais is sold as new wine although the 10 best wines from the area are not marketed in this way but are sold as *grands crus*.

78

Restaurant selection

The following suggestions from Burgundy's main centres
are listed according to three categories: $$$ = expensive;
$$ = moderate: $ = inexpensive.

Dijon
$$$**Jean-Pierre Biloux**, 14 place Darcy (in the Hôtel Pull-
man), tel: 80 30 11 00. Top-class cuisine with speciali-
ties such as veal kidneys in red wine and mustard sauce.
$$$**Chapeau Rouge**, 5 rue Michelet, tel: 80 30 28 10. An-
other first-class restaurant. Try the lobster ragout. $$**La
Toison d'Or**, 18 rue Ste-Anne, tel: 80 30 73 52. Marvell-
ous food, stylish setting. $$**Ma Bourgogne**, 1 boule-
vard Doumer, tel: 80 65 48 06. Good portions of regional
cooking. $$**La Dame d'Aquitaine**, 23 place Bossuet, tel:
80 30 36 23. Eat in a crypt. Good atmosphere.

Beaune
$$$**Le Jardin des Remparts**, 10 rue Hôtel-Dieu, tel: 80
24 94 94. Marvellous seafood and meat dishes. Superb
wine list. $$$**Bernard Morillon**, 27 rue Maufoux (in Le
Cep hotel), tel: 80 24 12 06. High reputation serving its
own specialities. $$**L'Ecusson**, Place Malmédy, tel: 80 24
03 82. Chicken dishes. $**Le Gourmandin**, 8 place Carnot,
tel: 80 24 07 88. Down-to-earth fare.

$$$**Hostellerie de Levernois**, in Levernois 5km (3 miles)
to the south of Beaune, tel: 80 24 73 58. Top-class Bur-
gundian dishes. Roast Bresse chicken a speciality.

Le Jardin des Remparts

Auxerre
$$$**Le Jardin Gourmand**, 56 boulevard Vauban, tel: 86
51 53 52. Excellent cuisine. Try one of the desserts such
as caramelised banana bread. $$**Jean-Luc Barnabet**, 14
quai de la République, tel: 86 51 68 88. Chicken a spe-
ciality. $$**La Salamandre**, 84 rue de Paris, tel: 86 52 87
87. Noted for its fish dishes.

Auxonne
$$**Virion**, in Les Maillys 8km (5 miles) away. Excellent
regional cuisine.

Service at La Salamandre

Nuits-St-Georges
$$$**Château de Gilly**, in Gilly-lès-Cîteaux 6km (4 miles)
to the north-east. Superb fish and meat dishes in an old
monastery cellar. $$**La Côte d'Or** (in the Hôtel de la Côte
d'Or). Sophisticated creations such as oyster ragout.

Autun
$$**Le Chalet Bleu**, 3 rue Jeannine, tel: 85 86 27 30. Burgundian and Provençale specialities.

80

Nevers

$$$Jean-Michel Couron, 21 rue St-Etienne, tel: 86 61 19 28. Menu includes grilled veal kidneys, mussels on a bed of raisins and other delicacies. **$$Le Puits St-Pierre**, 21 rue Mirangron, tel: 86 59 28 88. Traditional fare.

Semur-en-Auxois

$$Gourmets, Rue Varennes, tel: 80 97 09 41. Tasty, regional cooking. **$$Le Mermoz**, Route de Saulieu, tel: 80 97 28 28. Specialities include salmon rillettes with marc de Bourgogne and lamb.

Avallon

$$$Moulin des Ruat, on the D247, tel: 86 34 07 14. This high-class restaurant lies in the delightful Cousin Valley.

Sens

$$La Madeleine, 1 rue Alsace-Lorraine, tel: 86 65 09 31. Excellent, imaginative menu.

Tournus

$$$Restaurant Geuze, 1 rue A.-Thibaudet, tel: 85 51 13 52, fax: 85 51 75 42. Fabulous Burgundian specialities such as *quenelles de brochet* (pike dumplings) and Charolais beef. **$$$Le Rempart**, 2 avenue Gambetta, tel: 85 51 10 56. High-quality cuisine. Specialities include leg of hare in honey. **$$Aux Terrasses**, 18 avenue 23 Janvier, tel: 85 51 01 74. Popular restaurant serving high-quality food. Courteous staff.

Mâcon

$$$Les Capucines, 47 rue Jean-Jaurès, tel: 85 39 11 05, in St-Laurent-sur-Saône on the east bank of the river. The quality of the food exceeds that of the interior decor by a long way.

Active Holidays

Boat trips

The **Canal de Bourgogne** is probably the best known of Burgundy's waterways. It starts in St-Jean-de-Losne on the Saône and winds its way through the Ouche and Armançon valleys as far as Migennes on the Yonne. The prettiest canal is the 174-km (108-mile) long **Canal du Nivernais**. It links the Yonne at Auxerre with Decize on the River Loire.

No licence is required to hire a boat but the hire company must provide an official document which may need to be shown to the canal authorities. There is no charge for using the locks, but most lock-keepers are grateful for assistance when opening and closing the mechanical lock gates and a small tip is often expected. Some lock-keepers sell basic provisions.

For boat hire contact: Bateaux de Bourgogne, 1–2 quai de la République, F-8900 Auxerre, tel: 86 52 18 99, fax: 86 51 68 47; Aquarelle, Port de Plaisance, Quai St-Martin, F-8900 Auxerre, tel: 86 46 96 77, fax: 86 52 55 31.

For those who prefer someone else to do the navigating, boat trips and cruises on the Yonne, Loire, Saône and the Canal du Nivernais are available. Contact: Tourisaône, 1 place d'Armes, BP 93, F-21170 St Jean-de-Losne, tel: 80 39 22 61, fax: 80 39 22 04.

Ballooning

In fine weather, there is no better way of seeing the Burgundy countryside. Two companies organise trips, but advance booking is essential: Air Adventures, Avenue Général-de-Gaulle, F-21230 Pouilly-en-Auxois, tel: 80 90 74 23, fax: 80 90 72 86; Air Escargot, Remigny, F-71150 Chagny (south of Beaune).

Caving

There are three main cave complexes which are open to the public. The **Grottes d'Arcy-sur-Cure** in the village of the same name are just under 1km (½ mile) in length (March to October, daily 9am–noon and 2–6pm, tel: 86 81 90 63). The **Grottes d'Azé** in Azé near Cluny (1 April to 30 September, 10am–noon and x2–7pm; 1 to 31 October, Sunday 10am–noon and 2–7pm, tel: 85 33 32 23) consist of two sections. The first caves were used by prehistoric man, as weapons, tools and pottery have been found in them. These artefacts are on display in the Musée des Grottes. A subterranean river runs through the other section. The **Grottes de Blanot** near Cluny consist of 21 chambers linked by steep stairs (Easter to the end of September, daily 9.30am–noon and 1.30–7pm; October, 2–7pm, tel: 85 50 03 59).

Seeing it from the water

Up, up and away

Getting There

By air

The nearest international airports are in Lyon and Paris. Air France is the main agent for flights to France. Direct flights go to Lyon, just south of the region, from London's Heathrow (Air France has a fly-drive option on this route) and Manchester (Air Littoral, bookable through Air France). Geneva airport gives easy access to southern Burgundy. Air France Holidays (tel: 0181 742 3377) offer fly-drive packages to Lyon, including a variety of accommodation options in the region.

Travellers from America and other countries can get direct flights to Paris, Lyon and Geneva, although a charter flight to London, then onward from there may work out cheaper.

In the UK: Air France, Colet Court, 100 Hammersmith Road, London W6 7JP, tel: 0181-742 6600.

In the US: Air France, 666 Fifth Avenue, New York NY 10019, tel: 212-315 1122 (toll-free reservations: 1-800-237 2747); 8501 Wilshire Boulevard, Beverly Hills, Los Angeles, CA 90211, tel: 213-688 9220.

By rail

The quickest way of reaching Paris from the UK is to take the Eurostar service through the Channel Tunnel from London's Waterloo Station (tel: 44-1233 617575 from abroad; 0345 881 881 from within the UK). Travellers can continue their journey aboard the TGV (*train à grande vitesse*) on the Paris-Lyon line from the Gare de Lyon. It passes through the heart of Burgundy calling at Dijon (1½ hours), Beaune, Chalon-sur-Saône and Mâcon. Nevers can also be reached by TGV from Dijon; the line passes through Le Creusot, the nearest TGV station to Autun. Auxerre is not on a TGV line, but there are good rail connections from Paris (2½ hours) and Dijon (2¼ hours).

Tickets may be booked for through journeys from outside France. In the UK tickets can be booked from any British Rail station, including ferry and Channel Tunnel travel. There are several rail-only and rail combination passes available to foreign visitors. These must always be bought before departing for France. In the UK a Euro-domino Pass offers unlimited rail travel on any 3, 5 or 10 days within a month. Visitors from North America have a wider choice of passes, starting with the basic France Railpass which offers four or nine days' unlimited travel within a month. Then there are various types of Eurail Pass which offer varying periods of first-class travel throughout Europe; the Eurail Youthpass offers a similar deal for young people under 26. The France Rail 'n' Drive Pass offers a flexible rail and car rental package, while the Fly

83

TGV name plate

Rail 'n' Drive Pass combines internal flights on Air Inter with train travel and car hire.

In the UK information and reservations for all the above services can be obtained from French Railways Ltd, 179 Piccadilly, London W1 0BA, tel: 0171-493 9731; special information line, tel: 01891-515477; reservations tel: 0171-495 4433. British Rail International Enquiries, International Rail Centre, Victoria Station, London SWl, tel: 0171-834 2345.

In the US contact Raileurope Inc. on their nationwide toll-free number 1-800-4-EURAIL or in **Canada** 1-800-361 7425.

By sea

Several ferry services operate from the UK to the northern ports of France. All of them carry cars as well as foot passengers. Hovercraft crossings are fast, but more dependent on good weather than the ferries. The Seacat catamaran service offers the quickest crossing but, like the hovercraft, can only carry a limited number of cars. The port of Calais offers the fastest access by motorway to the region; other good alternatives are Boulogne and Dunkerque.

By car

Visitors from the UK also have the possibility of taking Le Shuttle, the Channel Tunnel service taking cars and their passengers from Folkestone to Calais on a drive-on-drive-off system. In summer there are up to four trains an hour.

From Calais it is possible to travel by motorway right through to Burgundy (A26/A5, which joins the A31 north of Dijon). Almost all motorways in France are privately owned and subject to tolls (credit cards are accepted). Keep some change handy for shorter journeys.

84

Motorways are privately owned

Rapid transport on the TGV

Getting Around

By train

Information on services is available from stations (*gare* SCNF). If you intend to travel extensively by train it may be worth obtaining a rail pass before leaving home (*see page 83*). Children under 4 travel free, from 4 to 12 for half-fare.

Train et Vélo: Bicycles can be hired from most main stations. On many trains, cycles can be transported free of charge in the luggage van. Free brochures on transporting cycles by train are available at all French stations.

By car

British, US, Canadian and Australian licences are all valid in France and you should always carry your vehicle's registration document and insurance (third party is the absolute minimum, and a green card is strongly recommended). The Automobile Club National will assist any motorist whose own club has an agreement with it. Contact them at 9 rue Anatole-de-la-Forge, 75017 Paris, tel: (1) 42 27 82 00, fax: (1) 40 53 90 52.

Britons must remember to drive on the right and that priority on French roads is always given to vehicles approaching from the right. The minimum age for driving in France is 18; foreigners are not permitted to drive on a provisional licence. The use of seat belts and crash helmets for motorcyclists is compulsory. Children under 10 are not permitted to ride in the front seat unless fitted with a rear-facing safety seat, or if the car has no rear seat.

Speed limits are as follows, unless otherwise indicated: 80 mph (130 kph) on toll motorways; 68 mph (110 kph) on other motorways and dual carriageways; 56 mph (90 kph) on other roads except in towns where the limit is 30 mph (50 kph). There is a *minimum* speed limit of 50 mph (80 kph) on the outside lane of motorways during daylight with good visibility and on level ground. Speed limits are reduced in wet weather. In an accident or emergency, call the police (dial 17) or use the free emergency telephones on motorways.

Car hire

Some fly/drive deals work out reasonably well on short visits. French Railways offer a good deal on their combined train/car rental bookings. Weekly rates often work out better than a daily hire and it can be cheaper to arrange hire before leaving for France. Most companies will not hire to anyone under 23, or 21 if paying by credit card, and the hirer must have held a full licence for at least a year. The major car hire companies have local offices in Burgundy's main cities.

No shortcuts

Congestion in Mâcon

Tourist office in Clamecy and visitors to Taizé

Facts for the Visitor

Visas

All visitors to France need a valid passport. No visa is currently required by visitors from any EU country or from the US, Canada or Japan. Nationals of other countries do require a visa. If in any doubt check with the French consulate in your country.

Tourist information

The French Tourist Board can supply information and brochures on all regions of France.

In the UK: Maison de la France/French Government Tourist Office, 178 Piccadilly, London W1V 0AL, tel: 0891-244123.

In the US: Maison de la France/French Government Tourist Office, 610 Fifth Avenue, Suite 222, New York, NY 10020-2452, tel: 212-757 1125, fax: 212-247 6468; 9454 Wilshire Boulevard, Beverley Hills, Los Angeles CA 90212-2967, tel: 310-271 7838; 645 North Michigan Avenue, Suite 630, Chicago, Illinois 6061l-2836, tel: 312-337 6301.

In Paris: Maison de la France, 8 Avenue de l'Opéra, 75001 Paris. Tel: (1) 42 96 10 23.

In Burgundy: Comité Régional du Tourisme de Bourgogne, Conseil Régional, BP 1602, F-21035 Dijon Cedex, tel: 80 50 10 20, fax: 80 30 59 45.

The following tourist offices are in the main towns can usually provide information about their region: **Dijon**, Office de Tourisme, Place Darcy, tel: 80 44 11 44, fax: 80 30 90 02. Daily, 10 April to 14 November, 9am–8pm, in summer until 9pm; 15 November to 9 April, 9am–noon and 2–7pm. Syndicat d'Initiative, 34 rue des Forges, tel: 80 30 35 39, fax: 80 30 90 02. Daily, 9am–noon and 2–

6pm, November until 5pm. **Beaune**, Office de Tourisme, Rue de l'Hôtel-Dieu, tel: 80 22 24 51, fax: 80 24 06 85. 1 May to 30 September, daily 9am–midnight, April until 10pm; 1 October to 30 November until 8pm, 1 December to 31 March, Monday to Saturday, 9am–7.15pm, Sunday, 9am–noon and 2–6pm. **Auxerre**, Maison du Tourisme/Office de Tourisme, 1-2 quai de la République, F-89000 Auxerre, tel: 86 52 06 19, fax: 86 51 10 27. Office de Tourisme, 16 place des Cordeliers, tel: 86 52 06 19. **Auxonne**, Office de Tourisme, Place d'Armes, F-21130 Auxonne, tel: 80 37 34 46, fax: 80 31 02 34. **Nuits-St-Georges**, Office de Tourisme, Rue Sonoys, F-21700 Nuits-St-Georges, tel: 80 61 22 47, fax: 80 61 30 92. **Autun**, Office de Tourisme, 3 avenue Charles-de-Gaulle, F-71400 Autun, tel: 85 52 20 34, fax: 85 86 10 17. **Nevers**, Office de Tourisme, 31 avenue Pierre-Bérégovoy, F-58000 Nevers, tel: 86 59 07 03, fax: 86 36 69 94. **Semur-en-Auxois**, Office de Tourisme, 2 place Gaveau, F-21140 Semur-en-Auxois, tel: 80 97 05 96, fax: 80 97 08 85. **Avallon**, Syndicat d'Initiative, 6 rue Bocquillot, F-89200 Avallon, tel: 86 34 14 19. **Sens**, Office de Tourisme, Place Jean-Jaurès, tel: 86 65 19 49. **Tournus**, Syndicat d'Initiative, Place Carnot, F-71700 Tournus, tel: 85 51 13 10, fax: 85 32 18 21. **Mâcon**, Office de Tourisme, 187 rue Carnot, tel: 85 39 71 37, fax: 85 39 72 19.

Currency and exchange

The main unit of currency is the French franc (FF), which is divided into 100 centimes (c). Coins in circulation are 20, 10, 5, 2, 1FF and 50, 20, 10, 5c. Notes are available in the following denominations 500, 200, 100, 50, 20FF. Outside normal banking hours, cash can be withdrawn from automatic teller machines by using a Eurocheque card, although a charge is levied. A maximum of 1,400FF may be drawn with one Eurocheque.

Try to use up any notes or coins before leaving, as converting them back to your own currency may be expensive. If possible, take travellers' cheques in French francs. Credit cards, mainly Mastercard and Visa, are accepted in most hotels, but paying with plastic cards may be a problem in the remoter rural regions. American Express and Diners' Club cards are not accepted everywhere.

Waiters expect tips

Tipping

In restaurants and cafés a service charge is always included in the price, but an additional tip is usually expected.

Opening times

There are no strict regulations for shop opening hours in France. In general, shops and banks in country areas stay open for shorter periods than the branches in town.

Banks
9am–noon and 2–4pm, closed Saturday and sometimes Monday.

Vases for sale

Shops
Shops are normally open Monday to Saturday 8am–noon and 2–7pm. *Boulangeries* open at 7am – even on Sunday – for the sale of fresh *croissants* and *baguettes*. Many small shops stay open for longer during the holiday season, but close earlier at other times of the year. Many shops also close for one day each week, usually Monday.

Many of the supermarkets and hypermarkets are open from 9am–9pm, but they often open later on Monday at either noon or 1pm.

Official buildings
Monday to Friday, 9am–noon and 2–5pm.

Post offices
The PTT post offices (*Postes et Télécommunications, Télédiffusion*) are open from Monday to Friday 9am–7pm (in country areas Monday to Friday 8am–noon and 2–6.30pm) and on Saturday until noon.

Museums
Most state-run museums are closed on Monday or Tuesday and between noon and 2pm. There are no fixed opening times for smaller museums.

Ask at the local Syndicat d'Initiative or Office de Tourisme.

Public holidays
New Year's Day, Easter Monday, 1 May, 8 May (VE Day), Ascension Day, Whit Monday, 14 July (Bastille Day), 15 August (Assumption of the Virgin Mary), 1 November (All Saints' Day), 11 November (Armistice Day 1918), 25 December (Christmas Day).

Maintaining communications

Postal services
Stamps (*timbres*) are available not only from post offices, but also small tobacconists (*tabacs*) and bars which sell cigarettes (*bar-tabacs*).

Telephone
More card-operated telephones are likely to be found than the old coin-operated models. Post offices and *tabacs* sell the plastic cards with 50 or 120 units. A local call costs 1FF and the cheap tariff for long-distance calls applies on weekdays from 6pm to 8am, Saturday from 2pm to 8am on Monday and on public holidays. The cheap rate for calls abroad starts at 9.30pm.

Calling from one *département* to another requires no dialling code for 8-digit numbers, other then a 1 for Paris.

To make an international call, lift the receiver, insert the money (if necessary), dial 19, wait for the tone to change, then dial the country code, followed by the area code (omitting any initial 0) and the number. AT&T, tel: 19-0011; MCI, tel: 19-0019; Sprint, tel: 19-0087.

To take advantage of cheap rates, use the telephone weekdays between 10.30pm and 8am and at weekends after 2pm on Saturday.

Time

French time is one hour ahead of Greenwich Mean Time and British Summer Time, apart from four weeks in the autumn when the times coincide.

Voltage

Apart from one or two exceptions, mains voltage is 220V. It is worth buying an adapter for continental sockets if you are intending to take any electrical appliances.

In a few rural areas voltage is only 110V, but some appliances can be converted to lower voltages.

Clothes sizes

Most shops will let you try on clothes (*essayer*) before buying. Children's sizes, in particular, tend to be small compared with UK and US age ranges. Hypermarkets have good-value children's clothes.

The disabled

A list of accommodation which is suitable for the disabled can be obtained from the A.P.F., Délégation de Paris, 22 rue du Père-Guérin, F-75013 Paris.

Photography

In many museums and castles, photographers must first obtain special permission, especially if a flash or tripod is to be used, and a charge is sometimes made.

The ultimate pose

Buying direct

You may be tempted by all the signs you see along the road for *dégustations* (tastings). Many wine producers and farmers will invite you to try their wines and other produce with an eye to selling you a case, or, for instance, a few jars of pâté. This is a good way to try before you buy.

Newspapers

Newspapers can be bought at kiosks, bookshops or in *bar-tabacs*. There are some regional newspapers such as *Le Progrès*, *Le Bien Public* or *Les Dépêches*. Foreign newspapers are available from newsagents and bookshops.

Sample some regional products

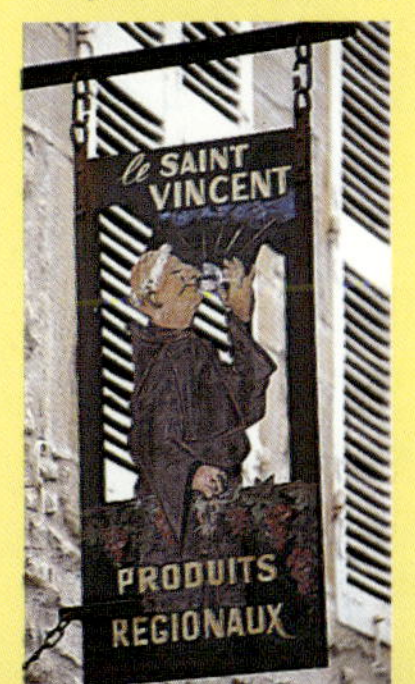

Medical

Visitors to France can expect to have to pay for medical treatment, should it be necessary. Although travellers from EU countries are advised to acquire the E111 certificate, which entitles holders to take advantage of health facilities in other EU countries, in practice not all doctors will accept it, preferring to make private arrangements with patients. It is therefore much safer to take out ordinary travel insurance which generally meets the full extent of any claim.

For minor ailments it may be worth consulting a pharmacy (recognisable by its green cross sign), who have wider 'prescribing' powers than chemists in the UK or US. Emergency opening times for chemists (*pharmacies*) are usually published in the local newspapers, sometimes in the tourist offices (*Syndicat d'Initiative or Office de Tourisme*) but are always on display at the chemist's shop.

In cases of medical emergency, either dial 15 for an ambulance or call the Service d'Aide Médicale d'Urgence (SAMU) which exists in most large towns and cities – numbers are given at the front of telephone directories.

Emergencies

Ambulance: tel: 15.
Police: tel: 17.
Fire (*sapeurs-pompiers*): tel: 18

Diplomatic representation

In most cases, the nearest consular services are in the French capital.

American Consulate, 2 rue St-Florentin, 75001 Paris, tel: (1) 42 96 14 88.

British Consulate, 9 avenue Hoche, 75008 Paris, tel: (1) 42 66 91 42.

The local gendarmerie

Accommodation

Dijon's Pullman La Cloche

Most hotels in France are accredited by the *Direction du Tourisme* and there are a total of five categories. Hotels which have been approved by the tourist office can be identified by a hexagonal blue plate showing the letter 'H' at the entrance. The number of stars awarded usually gives some idea of the degree of comfort that can be expected and also the price range.

For a list of all the hotels in the region, contact the Comité Régional du Tourisme de Bourgogne, Conseil Régional, BP 1602, F-21035 Dijon Cedex, tel: 80 50 10 20, fax: 80 30 59 45.

Neotel Transeurope

The 'Neotel Transeurope' chain of hotels owns many establishments throughout France. Its hotels, some modern, some more traditional, are located both in the town centres and on the edge of towns. The company prides itself on quality, hospitality and tradition. To help visitors who are touring the region, the hotel receptionist will be happy to reserve rooms at the next destination.

For further information, contact Neotel Transeurope Hotels, 78 rue du Moulin Vert, F-75014 Paris, tel: 0033 (1) 45678901, fax: 0033 (1) 45678901.

Ibis/Urbis

The Ibis hotel chain has over 200 sites throughout France – the Urbis hotels are located in town centres. Their rooms come into the two-star category and all have a bath, WC, colour TV and telephone. A generous breakfast buffet is available from 6.30am and children under the age of eight can stay free in the same room as their parents.

Ibis, 6–8 rue du Bois-Briard, 91021 Evry Crdex, tel: (1) 60 77 27 27, fax: 60 77 22 83.

Climat de France

Hotels belonging to the Climat de France chain are situated in most of the main tourist centres and are geared towards families.

Climat de France, 5 Avenue du Cap-Horn, ZAC de Courtaboeuf, BP 93, 91943 Les Ulis, tel: (1) 64 46 01 23 or 05 11 22 11 (toll-free in France), fax: (1) 69 28 24 02. UK office: tel: 0171-287 3181.

Logis de France

The hotels in the Logis de France group, identified by the distinctive symbol of a yellow fireplace on a green background, are usually smaller, family-run concerns, mainly located in country areas. Certain standards of accommodation are guaranteed and regional *haute cuisine*

Graceful residence

can be expected. The Logis de France guide is available from the French Tourist Offiice (*see page 86*) or bookshops in France. For the central reservation office in Paris, tel: (1) 45 84 83 87.

Relais du Silence

Expect to find these hotels in delightful, peaceful surroundings. The hoteliers are committed to providing high-quality regional dishes.

Secretariat Relais du Silence, 2 passage du Guesclin, F-75015 Paris, tel: (1) 45 66 77 77, fax: (1) 40 65 90 09.

Gîtes de France

France has what is probably the best network of self-catering holiday cottages anywhere in Europe. *Gîtes Ruraux* are holiday houses or flats, usually set in the country. The Fédération des Gîtes Ruraux de France monitors the quality of the accommodation. Standards are maintained in accordance with its 'star' rating (which in fact is shown by by ears of corn on a scale of one to four).

UK booking office: 178 Piccadilly, London W1V 9DB, tel: 0171-493 3480. A comprehensive guide listing all French *gîtes* is available from the French Tourist Office, as well as good bookshops in France.

Bed and breakfast

Chambres d'Hôtes are rooms in private houses which provide simple and cheap overnight accommodation similar to English 'Bed and Breakfast'. The house owners are members of the Fédération des Gîtes Ruraux de France and standards are maintained in accordance with the same classification as applied to the Gîtes Ruraux (*see above*).

Youth hostels

There are plenty of youth hostels in Burgundy. A full list can be obtained from the Youth Hostel Association. An international youth hostel card should be obtained before departure. There are two organisations in France:

Fédération Unie des Auberges de Jeunesse, 27 rue Pajol, F-75018 Paris, tel: 00 33 (1) 46 07 00 01, fax: 00 33 (1) 46 07 93 10.

Ligue Française pour les Auberges de la Jeunesse, 38 boulevard Raspail, F-75007 Paris, tel: 00 33 (1) 45 48 69 84, fax: 00 33 (1) 45 44 57 47.

Camping and caravans

The French Tourist Office (*see page 86*) will provide a free list of camp sites in France. During the peak holiday season, it is always advisable to make a reservation. One of the most up-to-date guides to French camp sites is the Michelin guide 'Camping Caravaning in France'.

Hotel selection

The following suggestions from the main centres are listed according to three categories: $$$ = expensive; $$ = moderate; $ = inexpensive.

Autun
$$$**Hôtel des Ursulines**, 14 rue de Rivault, tel: 85 52 68 00, fax: 85 86 23 07. Tasteful accommodation surrounded by a traditional French garden. Excellent poultry dishes in the restaurant. $$**Golf Hôtel**, Route de Chalon, tel: 85 52 00 00, fax: 85 52 20 20. Small but practical rooms. $$**Hôtel St-Louis**, 6 rue de l'Arbalète, tel: 85 52 21 03, fax: 85 86 32 54. Pleasant, well-run hotel.

Camping Municipal du Pont d'Arroux, on the RN80, tel: 85 52 10 82.

Auxerre
$$$**Parc des Maréchaux**, 6 avenue Foch, tel: 86 51 43 77, fax: 86 51 31 77. Luxury rooms, some with view of park. $$$**Le Maxime**, 2 quai Marine, tel: 86 52 14 19, fax: 86 52 21 70. Best hotel in town. Rooms furnished in rustic style. $$**Les Clairions**, RN6 (north), tel: 86 46 85 64, fax: 86 48 16 38. Clean, modern rooms. $$**Le Commerce**, 5 rue René-Schaeffer, tel: 86 52 03 16, fax: 86 52 42 37. In the heart of the old town. Attractive rooms. $**Hotel de la Porte de Paris**, 5 rue St-Germain, tel: 86 46 90 09. A modest hotel; only 2 of its rooms have private bathrooms.

Camping Municipal, 8 route de Vaux, tel: 86 52 11 15.

Auxonne
$$**Hôtel du Corbeau**, 1 rue de Berbis, tel: 80 31 11 88, fax: 80 31 04 59. Small hotel with only 10 rooms.

Some campsites are idyllic

Hôtel des Ursulines

Avallon Ambience

$Auberge du Cheval Rouge, 5km (3 miles) away in Villers-Les-Pots. Tel: 80 31 44 88, fax: 80 31 17 01. Basic accommodation with own restaurant.

Avallon

$$$Hostellerie de la Poste, Place Vauban, tel: 86 34 06 12, fax: 86 34 47 11. Well-run hotel in 18th-century premises. **$$Hôtel d'Avallon-Vauban**, 53 rue de Paris, tel: 86 34 36 99, fax: 86 31 66 31. Comfortable hotel.

Beaune

Hotel Le Cep

$$$Le Cep, 27 rue Maufoux, tel: 80 22 35 48, fax: 80 22 76 80. Luxury hotel in a Renaissance house. **$$$Béléna**, 10 boulevard Foch, tel: 80 24 01 01, fax: 80 24 09 90. New and luxurious hotel. **$$Le Home**, 138 route de Dijon, tel: 80 22 16 43, fax: 80 24 90 74. Pretty country hotel covered in grape vines. Out of town. **$$Arcade**, Avenue Charles-de-Gaulle, tel: 80 22 75 67, fax: 80 22 77 17. Pleasant medium-category hotel with swimming pool. **$Alésia**, 4 avenue des Sablières, tel: 80 22 63 27, fax: 80 24 95 28. Small hotel away from the town centre.

Camping Les Cent Vignes, 10 rue A.-Dubois, tel: 80 22 03 91.

Dijon

The Wilson

$$$Wilson, Place Wilson, tel: 80 66 82 50, fax: 80 36 41 54. 17th-century post house. Splendidly furnished. **$$$Pullman La Cloche**, 14 place Darcy, tel: 80 30 12 32, fax: 80 30 04 15. Dijon's grandest hotel. **$$$Mercure-Altéa Château Bourgogne**, 22 boulevard Marne, tel: 80 72 31 13, fax: 80 30 04 15. Luxury hotel with all the trimmings. **$$$Chapeau Rouge**, 5 rue Michelet, tel. 80 30 28 10, fax: 80 30 33 89. First-class hotel with magnificent restaurant. **$$Ibis Central**, 3 place Grangier, tel: 80 30 44 00, fax: 80 30 77 12. Chain motel. **$$Climat de France**, 15-17 avenue Maréchal-Foch, tel: 80 43 40 01, fax: 80 43 10 02. Medium-category chain hotel. **$$Le Jacquemart**, 32 rue Verrerie, tel: 80 73 39 74, fax: 80 73 20 99. In the old quarter. Very inviting and friendly.

Camping du Lac, 3 boulevard Kir, tel: 80 43 54 72.

Mâcon

$$$Altéa Bord de Saône, 26 rue Pierre-de-Coubertin, tel: 85 38 28 06, fax: 85 39 11 45. Three-star hotel with swimming pool and garden. **$$$Hôtel Bellevue**, 416 quai Lamartine, tel: 85 38 05 07, fax: 85 38 54 60. Pleasant accommodation in a centrally-located hotel. **$$Hôtel Concorde**, 73 rue Lacretelle, tel: 85 34 21 47, fax: 85 29 21 79. Not luxury accommodation, but quite acceptable.

Camping Municipal, 1 rue des Grandes Varennes, tel: 85 38 16 22.

94

Nevers

$$$Hôtel Loire, Quai de Médine, tel: 86 61 50 92, fax: 86 59 43 29. Excellent hotel with all the frills. **$$$Best Western Hôtel Diane**, 38 rue du Midi, tel: 86 57 28 10, fax: 86 59 45 08. Clean, well-run hotel. **$$Château de la Rocherie**, near Varennes-Vauzelles just off the RN7, accessible by a private road. Tel: 86 38 07 21, fax: 86 38 23 01. Nice rooms, excellent breakfasts. **$Hôtel Thermidor**, 14 rue Claude-Tillier, tel: 86 57 15 47. Basic, but large rooms.

Camping Municipal, Rue de la Jonction, tel: 86 37 56 52.

Nuits-St-Georges

$$$La Gentilhommière, 13 vallée Serrée, tel: 80 61 12 06, fax: 80 61 30 33. Modern accommodation in motel style. Spacious rooms. **$$$Hôtel de la Côte d'Or**, 37 rue Thurot, tel: 80 61 06 10, fax: 80 61 36 24. Small but fine hotel in the heart of the old town. **$$Hôtel Iris**, 1 avenue de Chambolland, tel: 80 61 17 17, fax: 80 61 26 33. Medium-category hotel with comfortable rooms. **$Hôtel de l'Etoile**, 5 place de la Libération, tel: 80 61 04 68. Basic accommodation.

Hôtel de la Côte d'Or

95

Semur-en-Auxois

$$$Hostellerie d'Aussois, Carrefour des Quinconces, tel: 80 97 28 28, fax: 80 97 34 56. Bright rooms with good view of the town. **$$Hôtel des Cymaises**, 7 rue du Renaudot, tel: 80 97 21 44, fax: 80,97 18 23. Pleasant medium-category hotel.

Sens

$$$Hôtel Paris et Poste, 97 rue de la République, tel: 86 65 17 43, fax: 86 64 48 45. Quiet rooms despite its central location. **$$La Croix-Blanche**, 9 rue Victor Guichard, tel; 86 64 00 02. Family-run Logis de France hotel with a garden. **$Hôtel de l'Esplanade**, 2 boulevard du Mail, tel: 86 65 20 92, fax: 86 65 95 75. Good value, friendly hotel in a central position.

Camping Municipal Entre-deux-Vannes, Avenue Sénigallia, tel: 86 65 64 71.

Tournus

$$$Le Rempart, 2 avenue Gambetta, tel: 85 51 10 56, fax: 85 51 77 22. Luxury accommodation with all the frills. **$$Hôtel de la Paix**, 9 rue Jean-Jaurès, tel: 85 51 01 85, fax: 85 51 02 30. Friendly hotel in a central location near the river. Good value. **$Hôtel de Bourgogne**, 37 rue Docteur-Privey, tel: 85 51 12 23. Reasonably-priced, with pleasant rooms.

Camping 'Le Pas Fleury', tel: 85 51 16 58.

Hôtel de la Paix

Index